D1246390

K I R K I E   M O R R I S S E Y

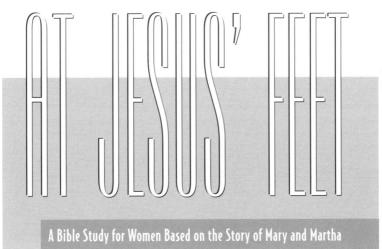

AT JESUS' FEET

A Bible Study for Women Based on the Story of Mary and Martha

LEARNING TO DRAW NEAR

"Martha, Martha," the Lord answered, "you are worried and upset about many
things, but only one thing is needed."

— Luke 10:41-42 (NIV)

NAVPRESS
BRINGING TRUTH TO LIFE
P.O. Box 35001, Colorado Springs, Colorado 80935

OUR GUARANTEE TO YOU

We believe so strongly in the message of our books that we are making this quality guarantee to you. If for any reason you are disappointed with the content of this book, return the title page to us with your name and address and we will refund to you the list price of the book. To help us serve you better, please briefly describe why you were disappointed. Mail your refund request to: NavPress, P.O. Box 35002, Colorado Springs, CO 80935.

The Navigators is an international Christian organization. Our mission is to reach, disciple, and equip people to know Christ and to make Him known through successive generations. We envision multitudes of diverse people in the United States and every other nation who have a passionate love for Christ, live a lifestyle of sharing Christ's love, and multiply spiritual laborers among those without Christ.

NavPress is the publishing ministry of The Navigators. NavPress publications help believers learn biblical truth and apply what they learn to their lives and ministries. Our mission is to stimulate spiritual formation among our readers.

FOR A FREE CATALOG OF
NAVPRESS BOOKS & BIBLE STUDIES,
CALL 1-800-366-7788 (USA)
OR 1-416-499-4615 (CANADA)

Contents

Acknowledgments

Writing a book is a team process! The team involved in bringing this study to fruition deserves not only recognition, but also my heartfelt thanks.

First I would like to thank my dear friend Ann Brosh, who for years has faithfully reviewed each study I have written before. Her input and prayer support has been invaluable!

Next, I would like to express my appreciation to the women in the weekly class I teach at my church, to whom this study is dedicated. Their input as we studied this book in its rough draft form, encouragement, and prayer support have made them a valuable part of this team. In addition I would like to thank those in Women ALIVE! who have had a significant role in this manuscript being submitted. June Libby initially encouraged me to contact NavPress. Her friendship and prayers have meant so much. My friend Elizabeth Alliman repeatedly insisted, "This study has to be in print!" Photographer and friend Deborah Killian gave of her time and skill in taking the photo used on the inside cover.

Last, but certainly not least, I would like to thank the staff at NavPress! Don Simpson initially gave a good word on my behalf to the committee considering my manuscript. My times over coffee and pie with Paul Santhouse, with whom I primarily worked, were rich not only in the dessert but also in fellowship and professional insight. I thank him for his listening ability, not only to my words, but also to my heart in all I desire to communicate through these studies. Additionally, I thank my editor Terri Hibbard, with whom I worked on the "nitty gritty." Each chapter was quite lengthy, so she had her work cut out for her (no pun intended)! And I thank my Project Coordinator Terry Behimer as well. It was a pleasure working with her. I also extend my appreciation to Nanci McAlister in Author Relations. All of the staff at NavPress has been very helpful and delightful to work with. I thank them most gratefully.

Introduction

The pleasure of your company is requested at the International Summit.

Dr. and Mrs. Billy Graham request the honor of a private conference with you in their home. . . .

Were you to receive an invitation similar to those above, how would you feel? Think about that a moment. What would your response be?

Actually, you are invited to an even more significant event with the living God Himself. Throughout Scripture this invitation is proclaimed. The King of kings and Lord of lords truly desires to confer personally and privately with *you*. You are important to Him.

As a young man, Isaiah actually met God face to face. Of this experience he wrote, "I saw the Lord seated on a throne, high and exalted, and the train of his robe filled the temple" (Isaiah 6:1). This encounter with the King of kings changed Isaiah forever.

It is this same Lord who extends the invitation to you, recorded in Isaiah 55:1-3:

"Come, all you who are thirsty, come to the waters; and you who have no money, come, buy and eat! Come, buy wine and milk without money and without cost. . . . Listen, listen to me, and eat what is good, and your soul will delight in the richest of fare. Give ear and come to me; hear me, that your soul may live."

Now imagine you have just received the following invitation:

The living God requests the honor of your presence for a private conference.

How do you feel? How do you respond? This is an awesome invitation.

Yet do you find it difficult to conceive of meeting with One whom you cannot see? Is dialogue with Him a real possibility or simply a figment of our imagination?

Many people down through the ages have testified to how marvelous and intimate communication with the living Lord is. In fact, God was so real and so wonderful to King David that David proclaimed, "I said to the LORD, 'You are my Lord; apart from you I have no good thing'" (Psalm 16:2).

Glimpses are given in Scripture of all that is offered to each of us in a vital relationship with the King of kings. But *how* do we nurture this relationship? *How* can we listen? *How* can we partake of all He offers? Because the Lord desires that we do so, He gives us insight and instruction throughout His Word, the Bible. Let us journey together as fellow pilgrims in exploring these exciting discoveries that await us, for Jesus promises:

> "Ask and it will be given to you; seek and you will find; knock and the door will be opened to you. For *everyone* who asks receives; he who seeks finds; and to him who knocks, the door *will* be opened." (Matthew 7:7-8, emphasis added)

CHAPTER ONE

Recognizing the One Thing

"Martha, Martha," the Lord answered, "you are worried and upset about many things, but *only one thing is needed.* Mary has chosen what is better, and it will not be taken away from her."
— Luke 10:41-42 (emphasis added)

Immediately Jesus made the disciples get into the boat and go on ahead of him to the other side, while he dismissed the crowd. After he had dismissed them, he went up on a mountainside by himself to pray.
— Matthew 14:22-23

Is there really only one essential thing for us to do each day? What did Mary know that Martha had yet to learn? Life offers so many ways to fill our days. In this new millennium, time has become such a prized commodity that people are making "Me Appointments" just to have time for themselves. Can you identify? Does the thought of making time for one more thing nearly push you over the edge?

Jesus understands the pressure of time demands. While on earth He was continually approached by crowds with great needs that only He was capable of meeting. He also knew the urgency of all He had to do and the brief time in which He had to do it. His mission was of eternal significance! By observing Jesus' priorities and what He taught Martha, we can discover His key to walking in peace and with purpose.

Time in God's Word
Martha and Mary's story is so well known that it is easy to overlook Christ's main point. Read this book's key passage, Luke 10:38-42, noting the

circumstances, Mary's activity, and Christ's response.

In *Then God Created Woman* Dr. Deborah Newman writes, "Martha, we are told, welcomed Jesus into her home. Many of us have done the same. We have welcomed Him into our hearts. . . . Welcoming someone into your home and sitting at His feet are two different levels of devotion. Jesus invites each of us to the level Mary experienced. He wanted that for Martha as well. He appreciated her welcome, but He wanted so much more for her."[1]

1. Why was Martha distracted?

2. What feelings or thoughts might Martha have had when Jesus said, "Only one thing is needed"?

3. In Psalm 139 David tells us that God knows each of us completely. What is revealed about Jesus' knowledge of Martha in Luke 10?

4. As we consider sitting at Jesus' feet, we must explore who He is and what, if any, authority and credibility He has. What do we learn about Christ from the following verses?

   a. John 1:1-4,10-18

   b. Philippians 2:6-11

   c. Colossians 2:2-3

5. What does Jesus claim about Himself in the following verses?

   a. John 10:14-15,22-30

b. John 14:6-10

6. What does Jesus reveal in John 15:9, and why is this important dimension of sitting at His feet?

Because Jesus is the Son of God and Savior of all who respond to Him, we know that we can trust Him. Because He loves us, we can be confident He will always have our best interests in mind.

7. In spite of the needs of those around Him, Jesus placed high priority on time with His Father and often set other things aside to guard that time. To document the kind of days Jesus had, read the passages listed below. Use the chart to record the context, the demands placed on Jesus' time by the needs of others, and Jesus' spiritual response.

Scripture	Context	Demands/ Needs	Spiritual Response
Matthew 14:13-23			
Luke 4:40–5:3			
Luke 5:12-16			

8. What do you learn about Christ's priorities from these accounts?

9. What lessons do you learn from Jesus' example about both the effort that's necessary to get time with the Father and the necessity of the time itself?

10. In light of your discoveries, why do you think Jesus says that "only one thing is needed"?

BETWEEN YOU AND ME

We always seem to find time to do the things we really want to do. I experienced this recently when a friend called with news of a great sale and asked me to go with her. My day was already full, but it was amazing how quickly I rearranged my schedule to make that sale.

What does this say about making time to be with the Lord? Through the years I have learned that apart from Him I can do nothing (John 15:5). He is my Life and time with Him is essential. Each morning I block out an hour to sit at Jesus' feet. I also take one entire morning a week for special time with Him. When someone asks to meet during these times, I respond, "I'm sorry, I already have a commitment then. Can we find another time?" Invariably we can. If Jesus felt He needed to spend time with the Father, how much more do we! Because He was able to make this time, we can as well.

Reflection and Application

English lecturer and author C. S. Lewis likens the importance of time with God for the Christian to the necessity of gas for a car. Author and Navigator missionary Ruth Myers develops this metaphor further: "Likewise, God made us to run on Himself. He is the fuel our spirits were designed to burn and the food our spirits were designed to feed on. So it's no use trying to find inner release and power and fulfillment apart from God. There is no such thing. And God has given us His life and power through our inner union with Christ Jesus our Lord."[2]

11. In support of this metaphor, what does Jesus state in Matthew 4:4?

12. How does Jesus' proclamation that "only one thing is needed" specifically apply to your own life?

13. A. W. Tozer, prolific author, scholar, and pastor from the mid-twentieth century, writes, "Modern civilization is so complex as to make the devotional life all but impossible. It wears us out by multiplying distractions and beats us down by destroying our solitude, where otherwise we might drink and renew our strength before going out to face the world again."[3] What practical concerns—whether large or small—distract you from sitting at Jesus' feet each day?

14. According to Oswald Chambers, respected author and YMCA chaplain to World War I troops in Egypt, "The greatest enemy of the life of faith in God is not sin, but good choices which are

not quite good enough. The good is always the enemy of the best."[4] In what ways have you seen this in your own life?

15.   What, if any, personal needs, demands, and/or responsibilities keep you from nurturing your relationship with the Lord?

16.   Read the verses listed below. What truth or promise is expressed in each one and how does it apply to sitting at Jesus' feet?

   a. Proverbs 20:24

   b. John 10:3-4

   c. Galatians 5:25

BETWEEN YOU AND ME
Realizing the Lord wants to order my days has been one of the most thrilling and life-changing truths for me. To see the Lord direct my steps has brought peace within and joy in Him. One reason many Christians have lost their joy in the Lord is, although they have given Him their *lives*, they have taken back their *days*. Because He knows the tasks He has prepared for us (Ephesians 2:10), the demands that are upon us, and our needs and priorities, He faithfully puts all in a good order. This truth

brings rest in the midst of busyness, imparts meaning to our days, and deepens our joy in the Lord.

Let me illustrate. One Saturday I spent time with the Lord and then gave Him my day with all the necessary "to dos" including grocery shopping. Intending to leave for the store, I sensed the inner restraint of His Spirit. As I turned to another task, I received an important, unexpected phone call and was thankful to be home at that moment. It was several hours before I received freedom and direction to go. At the store I encountered a woman whom I had not seen in years. She was obviously distraught in her spirit. When she saw me she broke down and sobbed as she poured her heart out. This conversation helped her at the time and soon she began attending Bible study, which helped her open her heart to the Lord.

Divine appointments. To see the results of allowing Him to order our days is a very exciting way to live.[5]

17. Recall a time when you were aware He had directed your steps, perhaps in retrospect. Write it here as an encouragement and reminder to seek His order for your days.

18. Read the Lord's invitation in Matthew 11:28-29. What is His promise to you?

19. What is your response to Him?

20. Ask the Lord to show you how you can make time to spend with Him each day. Record His answers. Then get your calendar and mark specific times to meet with Him. Determine to keep

your appointments. If someone makes a request of you for that time, simply reply, "I'm sorry, I already have a commitment then. Could we arrange another time?" If you were meeting a personal friend you would do that. How much more then should we prioritize our time with the living God!

In *The Perfect Love*, Ruth Myers writes: "In one sense [God] has no needs. But in another sense He has love needs. He has longings. And we as His loved ones can fulfill His deep desire through our love and worship, our fellowship, our obedience. This quotation captured that truth for me: 'Every soul is a vast reservoir from which God can receive eternal pleasure.' Each of us can bring Him joy in ways no one else can."[6]

Between You and God
The Lord knows and understands everything about you today, just as He did about Martha long ago. He also knows you cannot live life as it was meant to be apart from Him. So He calls you to sit at His feet—the one thing that is needed.

21.   Quickly review this chapter. What specific requests would you like to make of God regarding what you have learned? Write these beside the items below or process them with Him in a journal. As you progress through this study, review your requests and record the insights you receive. Topics you may wish to address might include:

   ▪ Distractions to eliminate
   ▪ Worries to let go of
   ▪ Truths about God to understand
   ▪ Desire to know Him better
   ▪ Wisdom to make decisions
   ▪ Relationships to improve

WHAT MAKES A JOURNAL?

A journal is a written record of your personal journey of faith. It is a place to write out your prayers and God's answers. To express your hurts and joys. To record your doubts and faith. To let go of the world and to embrace God's truth.

Two important guidelines in journaling are:

- Absolute honesty
- Total freedom of expression (find a secret place to keep your journal to ensure this)

If you hesitate to journal, relax. It's not hard. Write as if you were writing or e-mailing a friend. Simply express your heart to the Lord. Use pictures as well as words. Because journaling is just between you and God, develop your own style. My journal is a place in which I have poured out my heart to the Lord and have been powerfully met by Him.

CHAPTER TWO

Building in the Basics

"Righteous Father ... I have made you known to them ... in order that the love you have for me may be in them and that I myself may be in them."

— John 17:25-26

"Here I am! I stand at the door and knock. If anyone hears my voice and opens the door, I will come in and eat with him, and he with me."

— Revelation 3:20

Two people in a relationship are connected, share common interests, and interact with each other. By definition, relationships are reciprocal or mutual and cannot be one-sided. If a person claims to love another but does not receive love in return, he or she is not experiencing a true love relationship.

Relationships take time to develop and effort to strengthen. Much like living things, relationships do not thrive apart from being nurtured. They need emotional warmth and refreshment as much as plants need sun and water.

Trust or faith in each other is another aspect of relationships. This confidence depends on the character, ability, strength, and truth of the other person.

Thus relationships are built *on* common interests. They are built *by* mutual nurturing. And they are built *with* trust.

Think of the relationships you enjoy. How are these aspects demonstrated? What about your relationship with the Lord? By examining God's love letter to us, we can learn about the kind of relationship He desires with each one of us.

Time in God's Word

If we could listen to each other's private prayers, we would learn a great deal about each other, including our motivations, our hearts' desires, and true feelings between us. Likewise, if we could hear private conversations between God the Father and God the Son, we would discover the secrets of God's heart. We are given this opportunity in John 17 where Jesus' prayer on the night He was betrayed is recorded. Read John 17:13-15,20-26.

1. What do we learn about Jesus' motives toward us?

2. What is His heart's desire concerning His disciples—including those who believed during His lifetime, those who lived later, and those living today?

3. What are His true feelings toward those who believe?

4. Read John 3:16 and Matthew 22:37-38. What do these verses reveal about the relationship God desires with each of us?

5. Revelation 3:20 reveals more of the type of relationship Jesus is seeking. Based on this verse, what is Jesus doing for you and me?

6. What does He leave to our choice? Or what part do we play in the relationship?

Once a relationship is established, it must be nurtured. This is true of our relationship with the Lord and any other relationships we have. A. W. Tozer develops this aspect further in these thoughts:

> We have almost forgotten that God is a Person. . . . It is inherent in personality to be able to know other personalities, but full knowledge of one personality by another cannot be achieved in one encounter. It is only after long and loving mental intercourse that the full possibilities of both can be explored. . . . God is a Person, and in the deep of His mighty nature He thinks, wills, enjoys, feels, loves, desires and suffers as any other person may. . . . He communicates with us through the avenues of our minds, our wills, and our emotions.[1]

7. List all the ways you can think of to nurture a relationship. Are these applicable to relationships between people, between people and God, or both?

8. At the beginning of this chapter we said that relationships are built with trust. Why is this issue so important in relationships?

9. What qualities and attributes important to nurturing a close relationship with the Lord are addressed in the following verses?

    a. Psalm 44:20-21

b. Psalm 139:1-4

c. Psalm 145:18

d. Isaiah 29:13

e. John 4:23

10. We are often tempted to cover up our doubts and guilt about our sin. Why do you think this is true?

11. Read John 14:5-6; 20:24-29 to see how Jesus responded to Thomas's honest expression of doubt. What do you discover? How does this compare to how He could have responded?

12. What is Jesus' response to the open expression of guilt based on His parable of the Pharisee and the tax collector in Luke 18:9-14?

13. Based on Psalm 32:1-5 and 1 John 1:7, how will the Lord respond when we are honest about our guilt?

BETWEEN YOU AND ME

There was a time in my Christian life when, due to hurtful circumstances, I deeply struggled with whether or not I could trust Jesus to be totally good and always pure in all He said and did. As I wrestled with this, God gave me two insights which have impacted my life and my faith ever since.

According to the Scriptures, Jesus was "without sin" (Hebrews 4:15). John the Baptist proclaimed Him "the Lamb of God, who takes away the sin of the world" (John 1:29). Throughout Bible history, the sacrificial lamb had to be completely spotless and pure. To be the final, atoning sacrifice for sin, Jesus had to be perfect in every way—including every thought, action, and word. Because of the Resurrection, we know that Jesus' sacrifice was accepted (1 Peter 3:21-22). Thus everything Jesus said has to be absolute truth. So, because He said He is the Good Shepherd in John 10, He *has* to be!

The second insight is drawn from Revelation 4:11 and 5:9-14. At the end of time Jesus is worshiped for who He is and He receives or accepts that worship. As I thought about this important truth, I realized that if He had said or done anything from eternity past to eternity future that was not perfectly right and true, He would not be worthy of worship—nor could He receive it! In Revelation 5:13, I read that all creation will praise and worship Him in heaven by singing, "To him who sits on the throne and to the Lamb be praise and honor and glory and power, for ever and ever!" This peek into eternity emphatically endorses to me that *everything He has said and will say and has done and will do can be totally trusted as right and true.*

14.   What truths or insights from God's Word have encouraged you in your faith?

Reflection and Application

15.   In The Living Bible, the last part of Revelation 3:20 states Jesus' promise as, "I will come in and fellowship with him and

he with me." What reactions and responses to His "fellowship" do you have?

If you have not yet opened the door to Christ, ask Him to reveal Himself to you as you continue this study. Based on His character and the truth of His Word, you can be confident that when you choose to do so, He will grant your request.

16. How would you rate your relationship with the Lord today in the following areas? For each area, write a number from 1 to 10, with 10 being best. Use your responses to identify areas to pray about and to seek the Lord's help with.

___ Your sense of security in His love

___ Your obedience to His commands

___ Your awareness of His nurture and care for you

___ Your effort to nurture your relationship with Him

___ Your confidence in His desire to reveal Himself to you

___ Your trust in God's Word as truth

17. a. What, if anything, are you hiding from the Lord or afraid to share with Him that is consequently creating a barrier in your relationship with Him? Examine your heart. Ask the Lord to bring to mind anything you have been avoiding talking with Him about—whether it is doubts, fears, or guilt. Note these here or in your journal.

b. What doubts, if any, do you have regarding His character that keep you from pursuing a deeper relationship with Him?

c. What fears, if any, do you have that have created distance between you and God?

d. What guilt, if any, are you feeling? In each instance, ask God if it is true guilt due to unconfessed sin (Psalm 32:1-5) or false guilt due to Satan's accusations (Revelation 12:10). Take time to confess as God reveals. (Note: Because this is such an important issue, we will deal with it in more depth in chapter four.)

18. Review your response to question 17. What more do you learn about God's response to our humble confession of sin in Psalm 103:11-12?

BETWEEN YOU AND ME

In my journey with the Lord, there have been times when I have struggled with major doubts. One time we were being wrongly sued for releasing to the seller an option on some property. It was during a depressed time in the economy and the man with whom we had this option thought he could get additional money from us. Because there was no basis for this lawsuit, I was sure the Lord would resolve it. However, through many meetings, the man remained adamant. This suit was pushing us toward bankruptcy, but the man did not believe us. In my relationship with the Lord, at first I denied having any doubts or fears regarding His faithfulness in this matter. Every time I began to fear and doubt the character of the Lord, I would quickly stuff these feelings back down. However, the Lord knew they were there, and He cared.

Because He wanted me to be assured of who He is and be set free from the unrest my doubts were causing, He allowed this financial matter to reach a crisis. Bankruptcy appeared to be our only option. As I finally poured out my anger, doubts, and frustrations honestly, the Lord met me and didn't reject me. He was relieved I finally had come to Him. It was then that He was able to lead me into truth! He showed me the constancy of His faithfulness throughout the Scriptures, and He assured me from Hebrews 13:8 that "Jesus Christ is the same yesterday and today and forever." He also showed me that being faithful did not necessarily mean "nothing will go wrong," but that "he will never leave [me] nor forsake [me]." He will be with me "when I pass through the deep waters" (Isaiah 43:2), and will use all things to work together for His good purposes (Romans 8:28). Taking an honest look at my doubts and being assured of these truths set me free.

As I trusted God regardless of what resulted, the man suing us changed his heart and settled with us out of court. Yet even if we had been forced into bankruptcy, in my heart I confidently trusted the Lord and praised Him for who He is. This showed me how important it is to come to Him honestly, for it is then that He can truly meet us and set us free.

Whatever you are struggling with, *wrestle* with God about it and refuse to let go until He answers, even if this takes some time. Bring your feelings and questions to Him honestly. He understands and does not want you to deny your questions or to bury your doubts. He also desires to lead you into Truth. Keep seeking, for He has nothing to hide. Record your discoveries as you continue to process these with Him. For encouragement read Psalm 9:10.

Between You and God

19.   What truths of God's character are you absolutely assured of in your heart? Jot them in the first column below. If you start to write down a quality, but then hesitate, that reveals some doubt. Jot this quality in column two. Be thankful it has been revealed, and come to Him with it, seeking truth.

I am assured that God is . . .	I still need help knowing that God is . . .

Use this list as a source of praise and prayer requests. God desires that you respond to Him in love, spend time with Him daily, and trust in Him fully.

CHAPTER THREE

Feeding on God's Word

"Your word, O LORD, is eternal.... If your law had not been my delight,
I would have perished in my affliction.... Oh, how I love your law!
I meditate on it all day long.... How sweet are your words to my taste,
sweeter than honey to my mouth! ... Your word is a lamp to my feet and
a light for my path."

— Psalm 119:89,92,97,103,105

"The words I have spoken to you are spirit and they are life."

— John 6:63

GOD is the Supreme Communicator. From the very beginning He's desired to communicate with us—even to the point of becoming one of us. Jesus is called the Word in John 1:1. His very words are Life. Christ reveals this by calling Himself "the bread of life," and He states, "Man does not live on bread alone, but on every word that comes from the mouth of God" (John 6:35; Matthew 4:4).

The writer of Hebrews tells us that "the word of God is living and active" (4:12). His Word is powerful. God is alive and desires to speak to each of us through His Word today. When we come to Him through His Word, God uses it mightily in our lives. In *Transforming Grace*, Jerry Bridges clearly states: "The Bible is not merely a book about God; it is a book from God."[1] How absolutely essential it is then to read it, to study it, to feed on it.

Just as our physical bodies are sustained by eating food, so our spirits are sustained by feeding on His Word. But how can we feed on His Word?

Time in God's Word
A. W. Tozer writes, "The facts are that God is not silent, has never been

silent. It is the nature of God to speak. The second Person of the Holy Trinity is called the Word. The Bible is the inevitable outcome of God's continuous speech. . . . If you would follow on to know the Lord, come at once to the open Bible expecting it to speak to you. Do not come with the notion that it is a thing which you may push around at your convenience. It is more than a thing, it is a voice, a word, the very Word of the living God."[2]

1. a. Because Scripture is God's primary means of communication, we need to consider an important quality of God and His Word if we are going to trust it. Read the verses listed below to discern this quality.

  - Psalm 33:4

  - John 14:6

  - John 17:17

  - Titus 1:2

  b. What is the common thread in all of them?

  c. What unique fact is given in each of them?

2. What does it mean to you that in this day and age, there is somewhere you can go and Someone to whom you can go for absolute Truth concerning life itself?

3. What are we exhorted to do in 1 Peter 2:2-3?

A. W. Tozer also suggests that "the present neglect of the inspired Scriptures by civilized man is a shame and a scandal; for those same Scriptures tell him all he wants to know, or should want to know, about God, his own soul, and human destiny."[3]

4.   In what places besides God's Word do you see people seeking answers about life? Why do you think they go to these sources?

5.   In addition to His Word teaching us about life, what powerful claim about the Scriptures does Jesus make in John 6:63?

BETWEEN YOU AND ME

The impact of this truth was evident in a friend's life during a recent conversation. We were discussing her difficulty in making time to be with the Lord and to read His Word. As we talked about why we need such time, she realized she had never understood that Christ is her very life and that His Word nourishes that life.

Earlier she had talked about needing to get her kids involved in sports and the arts. As good as these activities are, they do not impart life to the spirit. She recognized she was neglecting the most important area. She exclaimed, "I really need to get them into Scripture and nurture their relationships with the Lord!"

She also applied this to herself. Up to this point, she had unconsciously been seeking life for her spirit by *doing*—primarily in activities in her church. She had everything reversed. Now she sees real life is in Christ. Her other activities are *outworkings* of that life rather than the *source* of that life. As she nurtures the life God has placed within her, she brings true life *to* all she does, rather than seeking life *from* the things she does.

6. Explain why you agree or disagree with the following statement: Many believers think they come to Christ for eternal life—but then look to the world for life in the here and now.

7. According to John 10:10, what is one reason Jesus says He came?

8. What significance does this fact have in today's culture?

9. These claims of Jesus show us the importance of saturating ourselves in His Word. What are some practical ways we can do this?

10. According to 1 Thessalonians 2:13, how did some first-century Christians respond to the message delivered by Paul? As we receive and feed on God's Word, what occurs within us?

11. Read 2 Timothy 3:15-17. What other properties of God's Living Word so you discover?

12. Carefully read the following quote from *The Inner Life* by Andrew Murray. As you read, number or highlight the workings of God's Word within us.

"All the treasures and blessings of God's grace are within our reach. The Word has power to enlighten our darkness: in our hearts it will bring the light of God, the sense of His love, and the knowledge of His will. The Word can fill us with courage to conquer every enemy and to do whatever God asks us to do. The Word will cleanse, sanctify, and work in us faith and obedience. It will become in us the seed of every trait in the likeness of our Lord. Through the Word, the Spirit will lead us into all truth. It will make all that is in the Word true in us.... "[4]

Reflection and Application

The fact that you are doing this Bible study is evidence that you place value on knowing God's Word. You have probably noticed there are some days when it is easier than others to find time to spend in God's Word. There are many things that can sidetrack us in this area even when we have the best of intentions. Remember Martha?

Tozer claims, "Whatever keeps me from the Bible is my enemy, however harmless it may appear to be."[5] This is quite a dramatic statement.

13. Reflecting on the verses we have looked at in this chapter, Murray's claims on pages 26-27, and Tozer's statement above, what commitment regarding feeding on God's Word would you like to make?

14. To help you fulfill this commitment, here are some pointers for getting the most out of your personal time in God's Word.

   a. Always have a Bible, pen, and a notebook or journal available during your study.

   b. Have a set plan of study (such as this one or perhaps a specific topic or book of the Bible). As you approach the end of one study, ask the Lord to direct you to the next one.

   c. Recall God's promise in James 4:8 and write it below. Personalize it by using "me" instead of "you."

d. Rely on God's promise to meet you—not your feelings—to determine whether or not you were met.

e. Prepare with prayer. Ask God to reveal Himself.

f. Focus on the Lord and what He wants you to learn.

g. Read aloud each passage in several different versions. Actually hearing the Word makes it harder to miss something important.

h. Personalize the Scripture, especially the prayers and exhortations of the Epistles. Read contemplatively without hurry. Try to get the true sense of the passage by asking simple questions like:

   ▪ What does it say?
   ▪ What does it mean?
   ▪ How does it apply to me?

i. Ask exploring questions like the following:

   ▪ What do I learn about God?
   ▪ What do I learn about myself?
   ▪ What does God desire for my life?
   ▪ What is my response to each discovery?
   ▪ How will I apply what has been revealed?

j. When God's Spirit stirs your heart with a passage, stop and meditate upon it. Savor it—spend time enjoying it.

k. Journal your thoughts and discoveries. Often it is as we write that He gives insights into ourselves, our circumstances, His nature, and our relationship with Him.

l. Throughout the day meditate on a verse, a phrase, or a thought from your Scripture reading. Ask the Lord to reveal what this means and how it applies in your life.

m. Memorize key verses so they become a part of you that the Lord can bring to mind when needed.

15. According to John 16:13, who is our true teacher?

BETWEEN YOU AND ME

My experience may encourage you in the truth that God's Spirit opens His Word to us. After receiving Christ as my Savior as a senior in high school, I attended a small college where I took secular religion classes. Things were being taught that I didn't think were true (such as denying Christ's virgin birth), but I had no one to whom I could go with my questions. As friends became aware of my faith, they began to ask me questions I also wasn't able to answer.

I had nowhere to turn for answers—except to God Himself and His Word. During the two years I was at this school, I poured over the Scriptures and was excited to discover how alive they are. The Lord led me into Truth and revealed Himself to me. I was thrilled. I came out of that time with a deeper love for Him and a greater excitement for His Word.

Later I attended Wheaton College and heard professors teaching the same truths that God's Spirit had opened to me as I sought Him through His Word. We don't need to be afraid of the Bible. The Author Himself meets us and reveals Himself to us through His Word. Such is His heart.

16. Use Colossians 1:9-23 to apply the tips for Bible study given in question 14 earlier. Review and do the first five steps. Then, continue with the following:

a. For an overview read this passage silently and contemplatively. Then read it again aloud, paragraph by paragraph. Record in your journal anything that initially impacts you.

b. Personalize the passage, using "me" or "I" for "us" and "you," and so on.

33

c. If something *impacts* you, stop. Answer each of the following questions based on Ephesians 1.

- What does it say?
- What does it mean?
- How does it apply to me?
- What do I learn about God?
- What do I learn about myself?
- What does God desire for my life?
- What is my response to each discovery?
- How will I apply what has been revealed?

d. Meditate on it. Talk with the Lord about it.

- What, if anything, makes you say "Wow!"?
- What truth stirs your heart? Savor it!
- What convicts you? Take time for confession.
- What prompts adoration? Spend time worshiping Him.

e. Write out your thoughts to Him in your journal.

f. Choose a thought or verse to meditate on during the day.

g. What prompts prayer for others? Take time to pray.

h. Choose a verse to memorize. Write it in your journal.

Andrew Murray says, "In your Bible study everything will depend upon the spirit in which you approach it."[6]

Between You and God

17.   Review Paul's prayer for the Ephesians as recorded in 1:17-23. Personalize it and write it out on a 3 x 5 card. Carry it with you so you can meditate on it and dialogue with the Lord regarding your heart in this.

18.   Paul gives a good view of Scripture to the Ephesians in Acts 20:32. Write it here or in your journal and reflect upon it.

CHAPTER FOUR

Dialoguing Through Prayer: Part One

> This is what the LORD says, he who made the earth . . . "Call to me and I will answer you and tell you great and unsearchable things you do not know."
>
> — Jeremiah 33:2-3

> Worship the LORD with gladness; come before him with joyful songs. Know that the LORD is God. It is he who made us, and we are his. . . . Enter his gates with thanksgiving and his courts with praise; give thanks to him and praise his name.
>
> — Psalm 100:2-4

"PRAYER is a dialogue between a person and God. . . . Prayer is as simple as talking to a friend and as awesome as being heard at the very throne of heaven," states Dr. Deborah Newman.[1] Amazing and exciting, isn't it?

Yet did you catch it? Prayer is *dialogue* with God. It is not a monologue or our talking to Him only. Throughout the Bible, God clearly reveals that He desires a give-and-take communication between Himself and His people. And He has not changed.

Dialogue involves not only expressing ourselves and knowing we have been heard, but also listening and hearing what the other has to say. The Lord desires us not only to speak to Him, but also to hear what He speaks to us. For God Almighty to make His thoughts known to us is an incredible concept. And yet it's true.

Exactly how does one dialogue with God? We will explore four key areas of prayer: Adoration and Confession in this chapter and Thanksgiving and Supplication in chapter five. To discover how to make prayer effective in your life, turn to His Word.

Time in God's Word

There are many examples of prayer throughout the Scriptures. Looking at all of them in this study would be impossible. We can, however, extract some principles and study them.

1. How would you describe your own concept of prayer?

2. How would you describe your prayer life today? Record a few key descriptors, both strengths and weaknesses.

3. In what ways, if any, would you like for your prayer life to be different? Express your heart's desires to the Lord.

4. According to Jeremiah 33:3, what is God's heart's desire concerning prayer?

5. What are you admonished to do in Colossians 4:2? What does it mean to you that you are called to this?

6. Within ourselves we do not know how to pray. According to 1 Corinthians 2:9-16, what has the Lord done for us to equip us to pray effectively?

The more we sit at His feet, the better we will know Him. In his book *Praying with Power,* Dr. Lloyd John Ogilvie expands this thought: "Prayer is more than saying our prayers. It is communion with the Lord who wants to give us His mind, guidance, and power. Most of all, He wants to give us the gift of Himself. He calls us into prayer to impart that awesome gift."[2]

7.   Carefully examine Philippians 4:4-7. What exhortation and promise are you given?

This passage from Philippians includes key elements of prayer. Bill Bright, founder and president of Campus Crusade for Christ, uses a simple acronym to describe these key aspects of prayer.[3]

A = Adoration: the honoring of God for who He is
C = Confession: agreeing with God about one's sin
T = Thanksgiving: expressing gratitude for what God has done
S = Supplication: expressing personal petitions and interceding
      for others

8.   Which words or phrases from Philippians 4:4-7 would you include in each of the four elements of prayer?

   ▪ Adoration
   ▪ Confession
   ▪ Thanksgiving
   ▪ Supplication

9.   In its simplest form, adoration is stating back to God what you know is true about Him based on His revealed Word. It is delighting in who He is. In Psalm 100:4, how does David recommend that we enter God's presence?

10.   Based on the following passages, what are some things about God that give us reason to adore Him? As you read these verses, give Him adoration for who He is.

a. Psalm 8:1,9

b. Psalm 9:9

c. Psalm 18:1-3,46

d. Psalm 23:1-3

e. Psalm 100:5

f. Psalm 111:1,7-10

11. Confession is agreeing with God's diagnosis and expressing our grief over our offense to Him. It involves turning away from sin and turning toward God. According to Psalm 66:18-19 and Isaiah 59:2, what is our condition apart from confession?

12. According to Dr. Ogilvie, "Authentic confession is to allow the Lord to press to the deeper levels of our lives to point out what He wants us to confess. So often we rehearse the surface failures."[4] Do you agree or disagree with Ogilvie? Why or why not?

BETWEEN YOU AND ME

Personally, I don't like feeling guilty. I don't want to feel bad about myself. As a matter of fact, I need all the affirmation I can get. Negative feelings are often the reason we avoid confession of sin. We don't want the Lord's penetrating light revealing unpleasant things about us.

Yet I have found that *authentic* guilt is good. It is the symptom that lets us know something is wrong—like the physical pain that alerts us to go to the doctor. In the same way, when the Great Physician of our souls points something out to us and we feel guilt, His purpose is not to condemn, but to save (John 3:16-17). He wants to alert us to sin so we can confess it and be cleansed of it. His penetrating gaze is always one of love and grace, and the result of His cleansing is life and peace.

13. Read Psalm 32:1-5 and 1 John 1:9 (see also 2 Chronicles 7:14). What does God promise to do when we confess sin which damages us and grieves Him?

If we do not feel forgiven after confessing, it is important to consider two factors. First, forgiveness is a fact, not a feeling. After confessing, we can rest in the assurance of being cleansed. The second possibility is that perhaps we have not confessed the "root sin" and that is why we still feel troubled. For example, we may have said something unkind, so that is the sin that we confessed. But perhaps the root of our words was an attitude of our heart that also needs to be confessed. Our desire, perhaps, was to hurt that person due to jealousy or a desire for revenge.

14. Confession is not a one-time thing, but rather a process of keeping a clean slate with God. It helps us to maintain open communication and to retain an unblocked relationship with Him. What are some of the results of an open, close relationship, expressed in the following verses?

   a. John 15:4-5,7

   b. James 5:16-18

Reflection and Application

Concerning the importance of prayer, Richard Foster remarks, "All who have walked with God have viewed prayer as the main business of their lives." He notes that Martin Luther declared, "I have so much business I cannot get on without spending three hours daily in prayer." Foster continues, "For those explorers in the frontiers of faith, prayer was no little habit tacked onto the periphery of their lives—it *was* their lives."[5]

15. Based on the amount of time you normally spend in daily prayer, would you say it is the main business of your life, a tacked-on habit, or somewhere in between?

16. Schedule an extended prayer time to sit at the feet of Jesus and to practice the concepts of Adoration and Confession. Right now is an ideal time to do this.

17. Begin with Adoration by reflecting on whose presence you are entering. The following list of names of God may be helpful.

   - El Elyon, "The God Most High" (Genesis 14:17-23; Daniel 4:34-35)
   - El Roi, "The God Who Sees" (Genesis 16:13-14; Psalm 139:1-16)
   - El Shaddai, "The All-Sufficient One" (Genesis 17:1-8; Philippians 4:19)
   - Jehovah-Raah, "The Lord My Shepherd" (Psalm 23:1; Ezekiel 34:11-12,15-16; Isaiah 40:11; John 10:11,14-15)

18. List attributes or characteristics of God for which you can praise Him. Pray this list back to God using phrases like, "Lord, You are . . . (specific attribute)" or "I praise You for Your . . . (specific attribute)." Relax in His presence, focus on Him, and delight in Him.

19. Read Philippians 3:7-8 along with the quote of Dr. Ogilvie following question 6 on pages **32-33**. In what ways have you seen this truth demonstrated in your life?

20. Move to Confession by asking God to reveal anything within you that is displeasing to Him. Confess those things you are aware of, any behaviors that grieve Him, and any actions you failed to take which would have pleased Him. Ask the Lord to reveal any "root sin" that motivated you in any of these.

21. Allowing Scripture to guide your prayers is powerful. As you read and meditate upon God's Word, His Spirit stirs your heart with His desires. Begin reading Colossians 1, praying as

Scripture prompts you. What truths stir your heart, particularly in the areas of adoration and confession? Pray accordingly.

22. This process leads naturally to thanksgiving for His promise of forgiveness and cleansing. How does the Lord see you, described pictorially in Zechariah 3:1-4? Take a few moments to thank Him for what He has revealed.

We will cover Thanksgiving and Supplication in the next chapter.

BETWEEN YOU AND ME

When reading 1 John 1:9, I was initially confused by the concept of a just God who forgives. It seemed that His justice would mean punishment, not forgiveness. Then I realized that because Christ paid for my sin—taking my punishment upon Himself—it would be unjust for God not to forgive me. By His very nature, He is bound to forgive. This fact has been a liberating realization, and it helps me freely confess my sin. Also, because He has paid for that sin, there is no need to carry the guilt of it! He has taken care of it and wants us to be free (Colossians 2:13-15).

An incident from my childhood which I carried into my adult life helped me understand this more clearly. When I was little, I stole a cute little clown key chain. I wanted it so badly that when my mom said "No," I took it anyway. Possessing that key chain made me happy for a moment, but the guilt caused me suffering for over forty years. One day I confessed my childhood sin to my mom. Her response was, "I know. I paid for it." Here I had carried that guilt for years even though it had been taken care of—paid for. How unnecessary my burden had been.

It is the same with our guilt before the Lord. We don't need to be carrying it. As we come to Him and confess our sin, He removes our burden with the truth that the penalty has been paid. Then we are set free.

Between You and God

Jeremiah wrote in Lamentations 3:21-23, "Yet this I call to mind and therefore I have hope: Because of the LORD's great love we are not consumed, for his compassions never fail. They are new every morning; great is your faithfulness."

23. Do you find it easy after confessing a sin to continue to "beat yourself up" over it? In light of this lesson and the truths in the passage above, what can you do instead?

24. What are all people to do according to Psalm 117:1-2? Considering who God is and what He does for you daily, give Him thanks and spend time in adoration of Him.

CHAPTER FIVE

Dialoguing Through Prayer: Part Two

"If you remain in me and my words remain in you, ask whatever you wish, and it will be given you."

— John 15:7

Do not be anxious about anything, but in everything, by prayer and petition, with thanksgiving, present your requests to God. And the peace of God, which transcends all understanding, will guard your hearts and your minds in Christ Jesus.

— Philippians 4:6-7

W HENEVER prayer is mentioned, we usually think of asking or receiving. This is where most questions arise. We read promises of "ask and you will receive," yet often our experience does not reflect that reality. Then we become disheartened in prayer and give up, thinking simply, "It doesn't work." Well, either God is lying, or we have missed something! If we remember that God is Truth, it must be the latter. In this chapter and the next, we will explore some keys to powerful prayer, shedding light on many of the questions that plague us. Having considered Adoration and Confession, let us now explore Thanksgiving and Supplication.

Adoration and Thanksgiving are closely related, but are very different concepts. In chapter four we defined Adoration as "honoring Him for all you know Him to be through His Word and in your experience." In contrast, Thanksgiving is our expression of gratitude to God for the things He has done or will do.

Supplication has two major parts: praying for our own needs (petition), and praying for others (intercession). In both cases we need to meet the conditions God gives in His Word.

Our approach in this chapter will be a little different because we want to spend more time applying the truths. Therefore the "Time in God's Word" and "Reflection and Meditation" sections are interspersed throughout the text. This material will be most meaningful if covered in an extended time of meditation and prayer.

We've seen the importance Jesus placed on prayer. As we place the same importance on communicating with the Father, our prayers will become effective.

This was demonstrated in the life of Dr. Hudson Taylor, a medical missionary who began the China Inland Mission. Author Colin Whittaker writes of Taylor, "The morning watch was one of the great secrets of his close walk with God and of his ever-increasing faith. No matter how busy he was, carrying out medical work, burdened with administration, writing scores of letters, or preaching, Hudson always made prayer his priority."[1]

1. According to John 14:13, what is a primary purpose of prayer? Is this a main concern of yours? As you approach the Lord during this prayer time, ask Him to accomplish this and to increase your desire for it as well.

2. Read James 4:3. Allow God to reveal any improper or selfish motives in you. Take time to listen. Then confess what He reveals.

3. What other hindrance to answered prayer is given in Isaiah 59:1-2? Having examined our hearts in the last chapter, review Psalm 32:1-5 and 1 John 1:9 for steps we need to take to eliminate this hindrance.

In chapter four we said that Thanksgiving is an attitude of gratefulness and a means of letting God know how much we appreciate all He has done.

4. Reflect on the verses below. List the spiritual blessings you have in Christ. Then spend time thanking God for all He has done. Include other favorite passages as a source of thanksgiving.

    a. Ephesians 2:4-10

    b. Colossians 2:9-10,13-15

    c. Jude 24-25

5. Read Psalm 104 for a partial list of what God has done and continues to do in His created world. Use this as a springboard to giving Him thanks for specific things about the physical world you enjoy. Record some of those things here.

6. What condition does God give for answered prayer in Hebrews 11:1-2,6?

7. What phrases in the following verses of promise clearly state the key to powerful prayer? (We'll study this more in the next chapter.)

    a. John 16:23-24

    b. 1 John 5:14-15

8. What concerns for yourself (petition) are you anxious about today? Bring each specific one to the Lord now. Unburden your heart to Him as to a friend. Take all the time you need to honestly process what is within, layer by layer. Realize that it takes time to peel back the layers of our minds, hearts, and spirits. Allow time to process these layers from *immediate* concerns to the *deep achings* of your heart. Like meeting a friend for lunch, begin your conversation with urgent or pressing issues and go on to your deep concerns within. It may help to journal your thoughts and insights. Write your concerns here or in your journal.

9. Ask God to reveal anything you may be holding onto or any area where you are being willful. Thank Him for all He reveals and process each area with Him. Continue to journal.

10. a. Now pray for others (intercession) including your family, friends, and anyone else God places on your heart. Write the name of each person and your area of concern below. Take time to hold each individual up before the Lord. Be still before Him as you lift them up. The Lord knows each of them completely: what is going on within each one, what each one's circumstances are, and what His purposes are for each of them. Ask for His insight, wisdom, and direction in prayer. Seek God's wisdom in how to pray for each, and then move on to part b.

Name	Concern	Bottom Line Request

b. As you pray for people, unless the Lord leads specifically, pray bottom line prayers or heart's desire prayers. Paul illustrates this type of prayer in his concern for salvation of the Israelites (Romans 10:1). Such prayers focus on the desired *result*—such as salvation, reconciliation, and growth in Christ—rather than *how* this is to be accomplished. The Lord reminds us that His ways are not our ways (Isaiah 55:8). So unless He leads in a specific way, it is most effective to pray your heart's desire— which will be His desire if you are abiding in Him. Effective prayer is not saying the right words but rather uniting your will with God's will. In this way you let God be God and open yourself to be surprised by how He may work! Look over your list again and then pray as He directs.

BETWEEN YOU AND ME

Bottom line or heart's desire prayers are very effective. I have seen women pray for someone for a long time with little or no results because they were praying *instructions* to God rather than focusing on the desired result.

For example, one woman had been praying for her daughter's relationship with the Lord to be renewed for years; but instead of simply requesting that, she prayed regarding ways for the Lord to do it. She prayed that the Lord would bring someone into her daughter's life to influence her; then that the Lord would lead her to a church; and so on. When this friend began to simply pray that her daughter's relationship with the Lord be renewed, the Spirit was released to act through the means God designed.

Eventually, the daughter renewed her relationship with Him, returned to church, joined a Bible study, and began nurturing a closer walk with the Lord that continues today.

There are times when we pray and it seems like nothing is happening. This may be because our enemy Satan is involved. The Lord can reveal this as we continue to seek Him. (In chapter six we will look in-depth at "Persevering When God Is Silent.") At this time, simply ask God to give you discernment about each person on your prayer list.

11. If you sense other dynamics are involved, consider the verses below. What do you learn about the spiritual battle in which all Christians are engaged?

   a. Ephesians 6:10-13

   b. 2 Corinthians 10:4

   c. Luke 11:17-22

BETWEEN YOU AND ME

I believe there are two dimensions to demolishing strongholds. The first is *binding the strong man* Jesus speaks of in Luke 11:21. This verse especially pertains to the person who does not yet know the Lord and on whom the Enemy has a stronghold. If you have been praying for someone's salvation for a long time with no apparent results, bind "the strong man" (Satan) in the powerful name of Jesus — then pray for the Lord to rescue your loved one. There is a battle going on and we need to get on the offensive to defeat the Enemy's purposes (Ephesians 6).

The second dimension is *demolishing strongholds* in the authority and power of Jesus' name (2 Corinthians 10:4). Again, if you have been praying for a change within someone or in a set of circumstances to no avail, ask the Lord for discernment as to whether or not a stronghold exists. The Enemy can establish strongholds through a variety of avenues including anger, fear, unforgiveness, rebellion, and many others. The Lord provides His weapons of prayer and the authority of His name to demolish these. *Then* His Spirit can work within that individual.

An example may be helpful here. A Christian couple was at odds about having another child. The wife (the daughter of my friend) was advised by her doctor not to have any more children. However her husband, normally a kind and sensitive man, insisted that she have one more child, even though he knew it put his wife's well-being in jeopardy. Several Christian friends prayed for some time for his attitude to change, but to no avail. The wife was just about to agree. As several of us met to pray, we were given insight that the husband's willfulness was a stronghold within that needed to be demolished. Using the divine weapons of prayer and the authority of the name of Jesus, we united in prayer to accomplish this by the power of God's Spirit. Suddenly the husband came to his senses and reversed his former desire. He was grieved over his attitude and asked his wife's forgiveness. As a result, they agreed to adopt a child, and they did so joyously.

12.   Ask God to reveal any situations where strongholds need to be broken down. Do not be in a hurry as you seek the Lord in this matter. Continue to pray until a breakthrough occurs. Consider enlisting others to join you in prayer as well. Sometimes the stronghold is so firmly established it takes not only time but the united prayers of others to demolish this. Take confidence in God's power over Satan and unite your will with His in defeating the Enemy (see 1 John 3:8).

As you finish this time of prayer, again thank God for all He has done and will do in the future in response to your requests.

Between You and God
Consider the following story and ask yourself if it applies to you.

A wealthy man loved his daughter very much, so he set up for her a "bottomless trust." Every time she made a withdrawal, the funds were replenished. She could never deplete the resources her father faithfully provided for her.

However this young woman was very busy. All the demands of daily life were too much, so she began ignoring some things in her life. At first the effects were not too noticeable. But over time her house fell into disrepair, and her clothes became worn and tattered. She knew she should be giving attention to these things, and they were weighing upon her; yet she just couldn't find the time to get to the bank to draw upon the resources her father made available. So she lived as someone in poverty, never using all her father had set aside for her.

13.   In closing, read Ephesians 1:3-14.

       a. What is yours in Christ?

       b. What does He desire for you?

14.   Finally, read Paul's prayer in Ephesians 1:17-23. As you reflect on this study and meditate on Paul's prayer, express your heart's desires to the Lord for your life.

CHAPTER SIX

Listening to the Spirit

Which of them has stood in the council of the LORD to see or to hear his word? Who has listened and heard his word?

— Jeremiah 23:18

"The watchman opens the gate for him, and the sheep listen to [the shepherd's] voice. He calls his own sheep by name and leads them out. When he has brought out all his own, he goes on ahead of them, and his sheep follow him because they know his voice. . . . I am the good shepherd."

— John 10:3-4,11

GOD speaks. We listen. A dynamic relationship and effective life result. Listening is an essential skill in discerning God's will which, as we saw in the last chapter, is the key to powerful prayer. Richard Foster in *Celebration of Discipline* says, "Attuning ourselves to divine breathings is spiritual work, but without it our praying is vain repetition (Matthew 6:7). Listening to the Lord is the first thing, the second thing, and the third thing necessary for successful intercession."[1]

Listening is also the key to productive living. As we discern what the Lord would have us do or say and then obey, His Spirit accomplishes the desired results. Listening transforms our lives.

However, the dynamic of listening to God's voice raises many questions. How can we hear and discern His voice? As you begin this chapter, take a moment to pray, asking the Lord to lead you into truth and to increase your sensitivity to His touch and the discernment of His voice.

Time in God's Word
1.   Occasionally we have heard it said about someone, "He says

God talks to him!" And everyone laughs. The message communicated is that the person who hears God is strange or not all there. What has your experience been in this regard?

2. Willingness to listen to and heed another's words depends on our view of that other person. What do you learn about God in the verses listed below? How does each truth encourage you to listen to Him regarding all your concerns? Be specific.

    a. Deuteronomy 32:4

    b. Psalm 145:8-9,13-21

    c. Isaiah 48:17-18

3. According to Romans 12:1-2, what heart attitude or position do we need to have as we come to Him?

4. As we abide or remain in this position, what occurs? Explain.

5. For further insight, read Joshua 5:13-15 where the "commander of the army of the LORD" stood before Joshua as the Israelites prepared to take Jericho.

    a. How does Joshua's first question reflect our thoughts as we come to the Lord at times?

b. Based on Joshua's response and his second question, how we are to come to the Lord?

6. Sometimes we come to the Lord already counting on our desired outcome. Other times we seek His approval of something that is very important to us. Or we may have no preconceived ideas at all. In what ways might our expectations and attitudes affect our ability to hear the Lord?

7. What example did Jesus set for us when He came to earth? (See Philippians 2:5-7.)

8. According to Lloyd John Ogilvie in *Praying with Power*, "We need prolonged times with the Lord so that we can experience the reorientation of our desires around His desires for us."[2] As we desire His will, of what are we assured in Philippians 2:13?

9. Based on John 10:3-6,11, what is Jesus' expectation regarding our ability to hear His voice?

10. How do you get to know or recognize Jesus' voice? Consider how you come to recognize someone's voice on the phone or your child's voice even among many others.

Becoming increasingly sensitive to the voice of God's Spirit is a process. At first, the Lord may need to communicate loudly and clearly so we don't miss His point. But as we grow closer to Him, He simply prompts with a quiet word in our mind or an awareness in our spirit.

11. When people have known each other for many years, they often know what the other person is thinking. They develop a "one-ness." In what ways, if any, does this reflect your experience with the Lord?

BETWEEN YOU AND ME

In today's society, courses on developing listening skills in inter-personal relationships are increasingly common. As we seek to lis-ten to the Lord, the Spirit provides His own training. As we per-severe, the Spirit increases our sensitivity until we easily recog-nize His voice and His touch.

An example of gaining understanding as familiarity increased occurred recently for me while watching the movie *Hamlet* (filmed in the early 1990s). Based on our son Mark's commendation of the outstanding acting, his wife Patti, his dad, and I agreed to watch it together. Because the dialogue was spoken as Shakespeare wrote it, we could barely understand anything that was being said. My husband soon gave up and found other things to do. I also was tempted to give up, but Mark's enthusiasm kept me working at listening and trying to understand. Patti and I soon discovered that the more we listened, the easier it got until it wasn't taking any effort at all. I was listening and understanding—and was thoroughly caught up in the movie.

And so it is when learning to listen to the Lord. At first it may seem difficult. Some get discouraged and give up because it takes such effort. But for those who understand its value and persevere, it becomes easier and easier. Finally, we discover, it's not taking any effort at all, and we are thoroughly caught up in the relationship.

12. How does this compare with your experience in learning to listen to the Lord?

13. What does Jesus state in John 15:7? How does this affirm your discoveries above?

14. In Jeremiah 23:16-18,21-22, what is revealed regarding the importance of listening to the Lord? What can be the results when we come up with a word on our own? (See also Lamentations 3:37.)

15. Why is listening key for powerful, effective prayer? Can you think of an example from your own experience?

16. a. As we seek God's wisdom and listen for His voice, what promise are we given in James 1:5-8?

   b. What conditions are placed on this promise?

17. When the Lord gives us direction—whether general or specific—what does He then expect of us according to John 14:21,23?

Our ability to listen with discernment grows out of our time at Jesus' feet as we fellowship with Him through His Word and in worship. We may hear His voice clearly in several ways:

- *While reading His Word.* A particular verse or phrase might jump out at us with clarity and authority, and be applicable to our unique situation at that time.
- *While going about ordinary tasks.* A verse may powerfully come to mind; or insight may be given through a "word"; or His will is simply impressed upon our spirit. (Examples of this are Acts 8:26-35, 13:1-3, and 14:8-10.)
- *While petitioning God.* We sense the Spirit's *yes* as we are making known our request. This may happen during personal or corporate prayer. (In a group, this is the agreement of the Spirit spoken of in Matthew 18:19-20. This agreement is not something we come up with on our own and agree to. Rather, as one is praying, others experience His *yes* in their spirits and then unite powerfully together in that prayer.)

18. Abraham is a wonderful example of taking God at His Word in Romans 4:18-21. What key phrase reveals the truth upon which our faith and inner rest are based?

19. Another dimension to effective praying is not asking but commanding. In this, the Lord empowers us to speak to an obstacle with His authority and remove it through the power of His name. What does Jesus promise regarding this in Matthew 17:20? Why must this be initiated or prompted by His Spirit?

Reflection and Application

Never give up! If on occasion you miss in this learning and discerning process, our enemy, Satan, will attempt to discourage you and prevent you from listening to God. He knows the value of hearing God's voice and doesn't want you becoming more sensitive to it. But the Lord is faithful. As you seek to hear correctly, He will give you understanding and clear perception. If at any time you do hear incorrectly, ask the Lord to show you how you erred and to teach you how to accurately discern.

20.   Has the Enemy tried to defeat you in this? What lies, if any, has he tried to get you to believe?

21.   Commit to setting aside a specific amount of time (at least ten or fifteen minutes a day) to seek God and to hear His voice. Write your specific commitment below.

22.   To begin this personal, reflective time, read 1 Samuel 3:1-10. Knowing that the Lord calls you and longs for you to listen, make Samuel's response your prayer as you come now into His presence. Write your prayer below.

23.   As you draw away to be with Him, don't rush or strive to hear Him. Don't try to make something happen. Simply remain in His presence. Focus on Him, and pray as things come to mind. Stay in His presence for the full amount of time you have allotted.

24. For what circumstances, situations, or relationships do you desire wisdom or guidance? Ask God to provide it according to James 1:5-8. In your journal, record each situation and God's answer.

25. What steps of obedience in action or in prayer will you now take? Be specific.

26. Review the concept in chapter five on pages 42-43 about holding up an individual before the Lord. Based on your answers to questions 25 and 26, whom might you hold up right now? As you do so, record any insights the Lord provides.

27. As we learned in chapter four, praying Scripture back to God is powerful because we know we are praying God's will. Select one of the following passages (or choose one yourself), personalize it, and pray it now.

   ▪ Ephesians 3:14-21
   ▪ Colossians 3:1-17
   ▪ Colossians 4:12b

Between You and God

In his book *The Inner Life,* Andrew Murray writes about the value and purpose of meditation. He states, "It is in meditation that the heart holds and appropriates the Word. . . . Meditation must lead to prayer. . . . The value of meditation is that it prepares our hearts to pray about the needs the Word has revealed to us. The Word will open up and prove its power in the soul of the one who meekly and patiently waits for it."[3]

28. Review the passages used in this chapter and meditate on one or more as the Spirit leads.

CHAPTER SEVEN

Persevering When God Is Silent

My God, my God, why have you forsaken me? Why are you so far from
saving me, so far from the words of my groaning? O my God, I cry out
by day, but you do not answer, by night, and am not silent.
— Psalm 22:1-2

O God, do not keep silent; be not quiet, O God, be not still.
— Psalm 83:1

B ECAUSE prayer is supposed to be a two-way communication, how dis-
tressing it is when God is silent. We seek Him, but He is seemingly
not there. We call to Him, but there is no response. The silence of
God is perhaps one of the most difficult trials to endure.

Is this unusual? Does this occur only when we have been willfully
disobedient and turned our backs on Him? Does He remain silent to punish us? Could He really have forsaken us?

In Psalm 34:4 David writes, "I sought the LORD and he answered me."
This, we think, is what should always occur. But does it? In the first place,
why would God be silent? And when He is, are we to continue spending time with Him? If nothing seems to be happening, is there any value
in continuing? Let's see what His Word reveals.

Time in God's Word

Not all discovery comes quickly and easily. There are times when God
desires to lead us into some deeper truths and asks that we *persevere* in
our seeking. The revelations of Himself are too precious to be revealed
lightly. In such times of struggle when He doesn't seem to be responding,

we are to keep seeking and not be afraid to ask the hard questions. He is who He says He is. He delights in revealing precious deeper truths and drawing us closer to Himself.

Christians throughout church history have experienced times of silence from God. This experience is often described as a period of darkness or time when God's hedge of protection has been removed. Responses during these times vary.

1. When have you personally experienced a period of time when God remained silent—when He didn't seem to be there? Describe that time, including what led up to it, how long it lasted, and your feelings in the midst of it.

2. A time like this is not unusual. Read the verses listed below and jot down the writer's name, emotions, and anything else you discover (or that surprises you!).

   a. Psalm 42:1-3,9-10

   b. Psalm 69:1-3

3. When we personally encounter a time of God's silence and distance, we need to first examine ourselves to see if we have distanced ourselves from Him.

   a. According to Psalm 32:1-5, what caused David's spiritual dryness?

   b. To restore fellowship, what did David need to do?

4. When God is silent and seemingly has forsaken us, we are responsible. Do you agree or disagree with this statement? Why or why not?

5. Read Job 1:1-13, then scan the remainder of chapter one through chapter two. What was the cause of Job's suffering?

6. For another example of God allowing suffering among His people, read Psalm 44:13-22. What reactions and questions does this incident raise in your mind?

7. For what reasons might God place one of His own in a position of suffering?

When suffering or difficulty invade our lives, we need to take the circumstances before Him and ask for His perspective. We need to determine if it is a time to stand against the trial or a time to accept it from His hand as a means of growth, furtherance of His purposes, or future blessing.

8. Based on Ephesians 6:10-17, what are we to do and how are we to do it?

At times when Satan is attacking, the Lord does not want him to touch us, so He directs us to bind Satan, rebuking the Enemy in the authority and power of the name of Jesus. As we do so, the Lord stops or prevents the attack.

Let me illustrate. When our son Scott was still in college, I was suddenly awakened one night with a strong sense that something was wrong and I needed to pray. For about ten minutes I prevailed in prayer on his behalf, rebuking and binding the Enemy in Jesus' name, and praying protection for our son. The burden then was lifted and as God's peace was given, I fell back to sleep assured that all was well.

Sometime later when Scott returned from college, he related to me that at around one o'clock that morning (the very time I was praying), the Lord intervened, proctecting Scott from a serious car accident.

9.   As with Job there are times when God does allow Satan to touch us (or something else in this fallen world). In these situations, we are to stand against the Enemy's intents while offering ourselves to the Lord for His higher purposes. According to Hebrews 12:4-11, what does God desire for us? From verse 9, what are we to do?

In *My Utmost for His Highest*, Oswald Chambers encourages us in times like this. He writes:

You will think that [your heavenly Father] is an unkind Friend, but remember—He is not. The time will come when everything will be explained. . . . Jesus said that there are times when your Father will appear as if He were an unnatural father—as if He were callous and indifferent—but remember, He is not. . . . Stand firm in faith, believing that what Jesus said is true, although in the meantime you do not understand what God is doing. He has bigger issues at stake than the particular things you are asking of Him right now.[1]

10. Because God is who He says He is, what are we to do, according to the following verses, when we are confused by the difficulty and He remains silent?

a. Job 13:15

b. Psalm 9:10

c. Isaiah 50:10

11. Paul tells us in Romans 8:28 that "in all things God works for the good of those who love him, who have been called according to his purpose." For each verse listed below, list the "good" He accomplishes.

a. Isaiah 45:3

b. John 15:1-2

c. Philippians 3:7-8

d. Hebrews 12:7-11

e. James 1:2-4

In his helpful study *Celebration of Discipline*, Richard Foster shares his insights about times of God's silence.

At some point along the pilgrimage we will enter what St. John of the Cross vividly described as "the dark night of the soul." The "dark night" to which he calls us is not something bad or destructive. On the contrary—it is an experience to be welcomed as a sick person might welcome a surgery that promises health and well-being. The purpose of the darkness is not to punish or afflict us. It is to set us free. St. John of the Cross embraced the soul's dark night as a divine appointment, a privileged opportunity to draw close to the divine Center . . . so that He may work an inner transformation upon the soul.[2]

12. How do Foster's insights influence your view of God's silences?

13. For insight into what God desires for us to do when we feel our prayers are to no avail, contemplatively read Luke 11:5-13.

a. What did the one persistently knocking finally receive, and what does this tell us about what God will do as we persevere?

b. What promise are you given in verses 9-10? (**Note:** The verb tense used in the original Greek reads as "keep on asking," "keep on seeking," and "keep on knocking.")

c. What further promise are you given in verses 11-13?

14. As we continue to draw apart to be with God when He seems distant and silent, what is He doing according to the following verses?

    a. 2 Corinthians 3:18

    b. 2 Corinthians 4:16-17

    c. Philippians 2:13

    d. 1 Thessalonians 2:13

Consider the following excerpts from *The Normal Christian Life* by Watchman Nee regarding times of darkness:

> There will be a definite period when He will keep you [in darkness]. . . . It will seem as though nothing is happening. . . . Seemingly everyone else is being blessed and used, while you yourself have been passed by and are losing out. Lie quiet. . . . Afterwards you will find that everything is given back to you in glorious resurrection; and nothing can measure the difference between what was before and what now is![3]

15. What thoughts or responses do you have to this quote?

Reflection and Application

We have discovered that times of silence in the Christian life are not unusual or to be feared. As they come our way, we need to continue to seek the Lord and His purposes.

16. What, if anything, is disrupting your communication with the Lord? Hidden sin? Ongoing struggle in a particular area? Disobedience to His revealed will? Whatever it is, take time right now to confess it. What will then occur immediately? Give Him thanks.

17. If you are currently in a time of spiritual darkness or a place of distance from God, take time to reflect on the truths—facts we can depend on—from His Word as revealed in the following passages. Jot down your discoveries.

    a. Psalm 103:10-12

    b. Romans 8:1

    c. Romans 8:38-39

    d. James 4:8

18. Now meditate on His promises in the following verses.

    a. John 10:28

b. Romans 8:26-27

c. Hebrews 13:5

19. Review the "Time in God's Word" section of this chapter for verses or thoughts you will hang onto in times of God's silence. List each here.

20. In times of silence, as well as in times of blessing, what are we to do daily according to Romans 6:13 (along with Romans 12:1)?

BETWEEN YOU AND ME

Offering myself to the Lord for the working of His purposes in me or through me does not always come naturally. I have found this to be a *choice*. There have been difficult times when I resisted God and fought against Him. There have been times when God was telling me to remain silent and wait for Him to act even though a situation was deteriorating steadily. As I fought against Him, my pain intensified and the unrest within me increased.

When I finally realized that the Lord desired to use the pain for good, I chose to submit to Him and offer my pain to Him to do the work in me He desired. No longer was my pain destructive; it became redemptive! God was using my pain to purge me of things that were not pleasing to Him—nor beneficial to me. This gave me peace in the midst of my pain. My prayer became, "Use this pain to accomplish Your good purposes within me." And He did.

Afterward, I found I knew Him better and was closer to Him.

My peace was deeper and my joy greater. Yielding to Him enables His Spirit to accomplish in us the work He desires. We discover that as we yield our wills to His, *His will actually becomes our will.*

21. If you have past hurts or unresolved prayer issues due to God's silence, take time now to offer each one to the Lord. Ask Him to heal the hurts, redeem the situations, and reveal Himself to you through them.

22. Perhaps you feel God is still silent. If so, seek Him and express your struggles or doubts to Him. As He directs, either stand against the Enemy and his intents or yield to God's refining. Persevere in seeking truth through His Word. Unite your will with His in praying that His good purposes be accomplished. In faith thank Him for what He is doing within you right now and what He will do in the future as a result of this dark time.

23. Express your trust in God or your desire to grow in trust. Also tell Him of your love for Him and your desire for it to deepen. Throughout His silence, rest in His love as expressed in John 15:9. Take time now simply to be in His presence and rest in the truth of His love for you.

Between You and God
24. Turn to Psalm 46 and read it aloud. Personalize it and read it again (for example: "God, You are my refuge and strength"). Now write out verses 1-3,7,10.

Ask God to increase your ability to be still before Him as you wait for His answers and provisions.

25. Claim Psalm 27:13. Seek to obey verse 14.

26. Be encouraged by the assurance you are given in James 5:11.

CHAPTER EIGHT

Growing Through Fasting and Feasting

"When you fast, do not look somber as the hypocrites do.... But when you fast, put oil on your head and wash your face, so that it will not be obvious to men that you are fasting, ... and your Father, who sees what is done in secret, will reward you."

— Matthew 6:16-18

Both high and low among men find refuge in the shadow of your wings. They feast on the abundance of your house; you give them drink from your river of delights.

— Psalm 36:7-8

HOW well acquainted are you with the spiritual discipline of fasting? The spiritual blessing of feasting? Would you just as soon skip the fast and go directly to the feast? Do you fear that knowledge about fasting will bring responsibility? What is your mental image of those who fast?

In Jesus' day, fasting was as much a part of religious experience as was prayer. In the eighteenth century John Wesley, founder of Methodism and a key player in the Great Awakening, revived the practice of fasting and "urged early Methodists to fast on Wednesdays and Fridays."[1]

Spiritual feasts were instituted by God when He gave the Law during Old Testament times. While these were feasts of actual food and beverage, they represented spiritual blessing.

Let's examine God's Word for principles regarding fasting and feasting which we can apply to our walk with the Lord today.

Time in God's Word

Fasting is basically abstaining from food for spiritual purposes. The word *fasting* in India is taken from two words meaning "dwelling" and "next to," or "dwelling next to God." Isn't that wonderful? Usually this is practiced privately by an individual; however, there have been public or corporate fasts throughout history, generally in times of crisis. This was an important part of the Israelites' lives done not out of obligation, but because they knew the benefits of humbling themselves before the Lord.[2]

1. What are your initial impressions regarding the practice of fasting today? On what are these based?

2. What do you think God's view of fasting is? What are your conclusions as you consider Joel 2:12-13?

3. Based on Matthew 6:16-18 and 9:14-15, what was Jesus' expectation concerning fasting when He was on earth?

4. For each passage below, list who was involved, the basic situation, the reason or motivation for fasting, and the result.

   a. Nehemiah 1:4

   b. Esther 4:15-16

   c. Luke 2:36-38

d. Luke 4:1-2

e. Acts 13:1-2

5.   Not only did individuals and specific people groups fast, but so did nations when faced with possible destruction. Read the Scriptures below and record the results of each fast.

   a. 2 Chronicles 20:2-4,30

   b. Jonah 3:1-10

According to Richard Foster, national fasts are not confined to biblical days. In 1756, the King of England called for "a day of solemn prayer and fasting because of a threatened invasion by the French." John Wesley recorded the results of this fast in his journal: "Humility was turned into national rejoicing, for the threatened invasion by the French was averted."[3]

BETWEEN YOU AND ME
Not long ago a friend called, asking me to join others in fasting and praying for a couple on the brink of divorce. The situation looked bleak because the husband already had an apartment selected. As believers united for fasting and prayer, the Lord intervened.

As the husband (whom I'll call "Bill") drove to meet with his attorney to work on the divorce settlement, he called my friend's husband "Don" to leave a message on his cell phone. Although Don doesn't usually answer his cell phone while in his office, this time Don felt prompted to answer. Bill was shocked, for he really didn't want to talk with Don! When Bill told Don where he was headed, Don boldly told him that what he was doing was not of God. He exhorted Bill that, instead of seeing an attorney, he needed to see a counselor to work on his marriage. Bill was convicted as Don spoke and his heart was changed. Instead of dissolving the marriage, his attitude became one of wanting to save it. As a result, this couple continues to work on their relationship and to experience a renewed love for one another.

6. As the above situations illustrate, the benefits of fasting are varied. From your personal experience, what benefits, if any, have you seen or heard of?

Dr. Bill Bright of Campus Crusade for Christ states: "God's Word declares fasting and prayer as a powerful means for causing the fire of God to fall again in a person's life. . . . As fasting and prayer brings surrender of body, soul, and spirit to our Lord Jesus Christ, it also generates a heightened sense of the presence of the Holy Spirit; it creates a fresh, clean joy and a determination to serve God. In short, it brings personal revival."[4]

Charles Finney, a powerful American evangelist of the eighteenth century, is an example of these truths. According to Dr. Wesley Duewel, Finney would spend "another two or three days in fasting and prayer whenever he sensed the work of God slowing down or less of the power of God on his ministry, and he testified that the power was always renewed."[5]

7. Which of the results described above would you like to see developed in your own life?

8.　Look again at Matthew 6:16-18. Based on this text do you think God is obligated to give us what we want just because we fast? Why or why not?

Consider Richard Foster's response to this passage in Matthew: "It is sobering to realize that the very first statement Jesus made about fasting dealt with the question of motive. To use good things to our own ends is always the sign of false religion. How easy it is to take something like fasting and try to use it to get God to do what we want. . . . Fasting must forever center on God."[6]

9.　If fasting has been part of your personal spiritual discipline, recall the reasons for these fasts and the results. In retrospect, what do you think motivated you to fast at these times?

When the word *fast* is mentioned, it is common to think of food. Contemporary Christian writers point out that other forms of fasting are also effective. According to Dr. Duewel, "fasting is a God-ordained form of self-denial. . . . We think of fasting as abstaining primarily from food. However, fasting may include abstaining from such normal activities as sleep, recreation, and other special enjoyments."[7]

According to Richard Foster, abstaining from sleep is called "watching," taken "from Paul's use of the term . . . [in 2 Corinthians 6:5]. It refers to abstaining from sleep in order to attend to prayer or other spiritual duties."[8]

BETWEEN YOU AND ME

The idea of abstaining from sleep for spiritual reasons has been a blessing for me. Now when I am awake in the night and am unable to get back to sleep, rather than becoming frustrated and resenting it, I offer it to the Lord as "fasting from sleep" in order to be with Him. Such times turn out to be very special. There are also times when I sense I have been specifically wakened by the

Lord to spend time with Him. I am always especially blessed when I yield in obedience to His call to prayer. I would encourage you to learn to cherish quiet time with the Lord in those wee hours of the morning when all is still. Instead of worrying about the impact of lack of sleep, trust Him for answered prayer and renewed strength for the day ahead.

There are two basic types of fast: absolute and partial. The absolute fast is the normal type referred to in Scripture where one abstains from "all food, solid or liquid, but not from water."[9] The partial fast is "a restriction of the diet but not total abstention."[10] In his book *The Coming Revival*, Bill Bright refers to this second type of fast: "The juice diet is the most popular form of the partial fast. [This] means abstinence from certain select foods and drinks, but not complete abstinence from all foods and drinks."[11]

10.   Read the following Scriptures and determine what type of fast was involved.

   a. Esther 4:16

   b. Daniel 10:3

   c. Acts 9:9

11.   What blessing do you think there is in simply offering our time of fasting to the Lord as worship and as an expression of our love for Him—not looking to get anything from Him?

12.   If we faithfully fast and nothing seems to happen as a result, has our fasting been in vain? Why or why not?

   Regarding unseen results of fasts, Dr. Bright says "a person usually has greater clarity during a fast, and sees spiritual needs and comprehends God's Word on a deeper level. . . . [However] some report no particular results at all. . . . I believe the Lord is especially honored by those who are faithful when no light shines through."12

13.   Just as fasting is proclaimed in Scripture, so is feasting. Feasting was a practice instituted by God in celebration of His faithfulness. For an overview of the feasts God ordained, see Leviticus 23. What words or phrases in this chapter express the importance of these feasts to God?

14.   Feasting is sometimes a result of our fasting, but also can occur through worship, simply spending time with Him in His Word, or celebrating how He has worked in a specific situation. What do you learn about feasting from these verses?

   a. Psalm 23:5

   b. Psalm 36:5-9

   c. Song of Songs (Solomon) 2:3-4

   d. Isaiah 58:14

   e. Jeremiah 31:12-14

15. According to Isaiah 25:6-8, Luke 14:15, and Revelation 19:9, what will the Lord prepare for us at the end of time?

Reflection and Application

16. Have you ever fasted? Why or why not? If so, what did you discover from that experience?

Because fasting can take on virtually any form of self-denial, it is also meaningful to have *spontaneous* fasts. There are two dimensions to this type of fast:

- At the time we are desiring a particular food, a special pleasure, or a material item, we choose to deny ourselves of it. We express our heart to the Lord—that our real hunger is for Him; that our true source of joy is Himself; and that our greatest need is Him.
- We can also do this as intercession. As someone we care about is hurting, we can deny ourselves a pleasure as a means of aching with them and for them in God's presence.

17. Would you like to initiate a spontaneous fast right now? If so, express to the Lord its purpose. Record your decision and request here.

Dr. Wesley Duewel makes these practical suggestions for fasting:

- Fast for a meal occasionally, and spend the mealtime (and, if possible, additional time) in prayer.
- Pray about planning for fasting as a regular part of your devotional

life—one meal a month or perhaps one day a month . . . or one or two meals each week.

- Spend the first part of your time feasting on God's Word, worshiping, adoring, and praising the Lord. Then concentrate on one or perhaps two major prayer concerns.
- Be flexible in your fasting. Avoid legalistic bondage, and don't take a vow concerning fasting. Rather, set a fasting goal that you seek to fulfill by God's help.
- Do not attempt long fasts (twenty to forty days) unless you have been informed how to do it and how to break the fast at the close. . . . Keep drinking liquids, for the body needs water.
- Keep a listening ear for the Lord's guidance when He calls you to a special fast for a particular need.
- Keep your fasting a matter between you and God alone.[13] (Unless you feel God wants you to share it.)

In addition to these suggestions, I suggest that especially for an extended fast (more than a day) you check with your physician first. And if you have any conditions that preclude you from fasting from meals, perhaps try a limited fast—give up unnecessary between-meal snacks or sacrifice a favorite food for a set amount of time.

18.   Perhaps God is burdening you to a longer fast for something He has put on your heart. Perhaps it is for a particular need of your own or that of another person; or for the church today; or for our country. If you sense His call, what is your response?

19.   After you have completed your fast, record in your journal anything that occurred in that time.

Prayer and fasting are integrally-related practices. In fact, Dr. Bill Bright, founder of Campus Crusade for Christ, says that his mother used to tell him "praying and fasting were two wings of the same bird."[14]

20.   In light of this fact, it is helpful to use personalized Scripture as a prayer to prepare for a fast or during a fast. Consider

Matthew 5:1-10, 6:16-34, and 7:7-12. As you read through these passages now, what stirs your heart?

Best-selling author Henri Nouwen commented, "When I think about the ways in which Jesus describes God's kingdom, a joyful banquet is often at its center. . . . This invitation to a meal is an invitation to intimacy with God."[15]

21. What do you think it means to feast on the riches of the Lord?

22. In your relationship with the Lord, have you learned to feast on the riches of Christ? If not, do you desire to know Him intimately and feast upon Him? Express your heart to Him here or in your journal.

23. What invitation is each of us given in Revelation 22:17? What is your response?

24. Fortunately, we do not have to wait for the Marriage Supper to partake of some of the riches of Christ. Read Acts 2:14-39, 1 Peter 1:1-9, and 2 Peter 1:2-4 and write down all the morsels you can feast on right now. Thank Him for each one.

Between You and God

For a time of feasting, read Psalm 111 in a spirit of praise and worship. After each verse, add your own specifics of how you have seen Him do that or be that in your life. Celebrate Him! Savor who He is! Use hymns of praise to supplement this time. Record your personal praises here to delight the Lord now and to encourage you in the future.

CHAPTER NINE

Enjoying God in Worship

Come, let us bow down in worship, let us kneel before the LORD our Maker; for he is our God and we are the people of his pasture, the flock under his care.

— Psalm 95:6-7

"Yet a time is coming and has now come when the true worshipers will worship the Father in spirit and truth, for they are the kind of worshipers the Father seeks."

— John 4:23

OW would you define worship? When do you think it should take place? Is worship something to be done only in church on Sunday? Or is it meant to be an integral part of a daily walk with God? Is worship a ritual to be performed or a response to God for who He is?

Do you recognize that the Lord is worthy of your worship and reverence? The word *worship* implies "worthship." Our Lord is totally good, completely faithful, absolutely pure, infinitely holy. He is King of kings and Lord of lords! In Revelation 4:10-11 we have a glimpse of believers at the end of time laying their crowns before Him and proclaiming, "You are worthy, our Lord and God, to receive glory and honor and power" (verse 11).

Because He is worthy of worship, God actually desires to be worshiped. According to Jesus, the Father actually seeks true worshipers (John 4:23). As believers we long to see the glory of God, and even more, to be invaded by His glory. Let's turn to God's Word to begin this adventure in worship.

Time in God's Word

In his book *Real Worship*, Warren Wiersbe uses the phrase "adoring response" to describe worship. He says he likes this phrase because, "It reminds me that worship is personal and passionate, not formal and cold; and that it is our response to the living God, voluntarily offered to Him as He has offered Himself to us."[1]

1. Who is the Lord according to Psalm 24:7-10?

2. How is God's glory revealed in the passages below?

    a. Exodus 40:34-38

    b. Psalm 19:1

    c. Matthew 17:1-8

    d. Revelation 21:23-24

3. In response to the crowd's praise, what did Jesus say in Luke 19:37-40? What truth about worship do His words communicate?

Worship is a natural response to seeing God! Two important aspects of worship—Adoration and Thanksgiving—have been studied in earlier chapters. In review, adoration is a response to knowing and loving the Lord for who He is. In contrast, thanksgiving is an expression of appreciation for what He has done. The more time we spend with Him, the better we know Him, and the more we enjoy Him. Enjoying Him is a result of being with Him. Together these things comprise a total worship experience that delights His heart.

We are to worship the Lord for His sake alone, not just for what He gives to us and does for us. Failure to understand this can grieve our Lord according to A. W. Tozer, who said, "I think God is disappointed because we make Him to be no more than a source of what we want."[2] How sad to confuse the gifts with the Giver.

4. Based on John 5:39-40, 7:37-39, and 15:9, what is the key to growing in our praise, worship, adoration, and enjoyment of Him?

5. Praise and worship bring the glory and power of God upon us. How is this evidenced in 2 Chronicles 5:13-14?

6. In *Mighty Prevailing Prayer,* Dr. Wesley Duewel also sees a relationship between praise and the manifestation of God's power. He writes, "God's praise seems in a special way to call Him to be active among His people, calling forth the manifestation and use of His almighty power."[3] How is this truth seen in 2 Chronicles 20:15-23? How can we apply this principle today?

Not only does praise invoke God's presence, it defeats Satan. Ruth Myers endorses this in *31 Days of Praise:*

As you pray and praise the Lord, you can free God to reveal His power as well as His presence. . . . Praise is a powerful weapon against Satan. . . . Any praise thwarts Satan. But to make your praise even more powerful against him, couple it with God's Word, and especially with truths that magnify Jesus as Victor. . . . Through praise we can defeat our Enemy; we can thwart his purposes and advance the purposes of our wonderful Lord.[4]

As praise defeats Satan, it also dispels darkness within. Praise is a powerful weapon.

7.   According to Hebrews 13:15 what offering can we give God? Why do you think it is called this?

Another aspect of worship stated by Ruth Myers is: "Through praising and thanking God, you put your stamp of approval on His unseen purposes. You do this not because you can figure out the specific whys or hows, but because you trust His love and wisdom."[5]

8.   Read the verses below and record what God's servants determine to do in each one. What significant things do these verses say about praise?

a. Psalm 34:1

b. Habakkuk 3:17-19

Although God created us with the capacity and ability to worship, that doesn't mean it always comes naturally. According to Ruth Myers, "You must choose to cultivate the habit of praise. . . . God doesn't enjoy your praise on the basis of how warm and happy you're feeling. As C. S. Lewis said, we may honor God more in our low times than in our peak times. You may bring Him special joy when you find yourself depressed or wiped out emotionally—when you look around at a world from which God seems to have vanished, and you choose to trust Him and praise Him in spite of how you feel."[6]

9.   In addition to pleasing God, defeating Satan, and strengthening us, what else does our worship accomplish, according to 2 Corinthians 3:18?

Author and Bible teacher Warren Wiersbe explains the concept of transformation by investigating the original Greek. He writes, "The Greek word *metamorphoumai* means 'to be changed into another form,' but this change comes from within. In other words, the change on the outside is the normal and natural expression of the nature on the inside. You would never produce a butterfly by pinning wings on a worm!"

Wiersbe relates this idea to the Lord's transfiguration: "He was transformed on the outside by revealing the glory that was on the inside. . . . It is this kind of experience to which you and I are called by God. . . . Every Christian is either a 'conformer' or a 'transformer.' We are either fashioning our lives by pressure from without, or we are transforming our lives by power from within. The difference is—worship."[7]

10.   Moses' encounter with God on Mount Sinai affirms these truths (Exodus 34:29-35). Based on this passage and 2 Corinthians 3:18, as you worship at His feet, what will begin to occur?

BETWEEN YOU AND ME
A friend once shared her experience of personal worship with me. It was a good example of the results of worship. She realized that worship was not a vital part of her relationship with the Lord,

but she desired it to be. In her first attempts to worship, she ran out of things to say after a only few minutes. Determined to develop her worship skills, she set a timer and told the Lord she was going to sit in His presence for the entire set time and it was up to Him to teach her to worship. Initially she set the timer for five minutes, then ten, and so on until she was regularly spending about an hour a day in worship.

"It's wonderful!" she exclaimed. Her husband added that after spending a day in personal retreat worshipping the Lord, she returned radiant—her face truly glowed! Worship has transformed her life and her relationship with the Lord.

11. According to Romans 12:1-2, what is our highest act of worship? What are the results of this worship?

12. Richard Foster indicates that worship is a catalyst of change. He says, "If worship does not propel us into greater obedience, it has not been worship. Just as worship begins in holy expectancy, it ends in holy obedience."[8] How does Isaiah's experience document this in Isaiah 6:1-8?

Reflection and Application

13. We have seen that God desires that we worship Him at all times in all things (see Hebrews 13:15). Prayerfully examine your personal times of worship. Record what God reveals to you. Complete these evaluative statements:

a. I am more likely to praise God in . . .

b. I am most likely to seek the Lord in worship when things . . .

c. My spiritual walk today compared to a year or two ago is . . .

d. When I consider spending extended time in worship I feel . . .

e. Instead of nurturing my relationship with the Lord, I find it easier to put my energies into . . .

f. Circumstances in my life right now that make it hard for me to worship include . . .

g. What do your responses above reveal to you? What changes would you like to make?

14. If you find your worship is dependent upon circumstances or if you are involved in a particular spiritual battle and find it hard to worship, bring these discoveries to the Lord and lift your eyes to Jesus. As you focus on the truths of who He is and how perfect His power is, praise Him. As you do, what do you discover?

The power of worship was demonstrated in the life of a friend as she decided to follow David's example of constant, persistent praise in Psalm 34:1. Over a period of years she kept repeating this verse while suffering in an abusive marriage and then through a painful divorce. As she did so, she stressed the italicized words: "I *will* extol the Lord at *all* times; his praise *will always* be on my lips." In the midst of the trial, she *chose* to praise God even when she didn't feel like it. She worshiped Him because she knew who He is. Her attitude greatly impacted me. She shared that she experienced a renewing of her strength as she chose to worship during this time. She testified that this enabled her to make it; and she not only survived, she overcame! Her face radiated joy (and it was evident that it came from deep within) even while her heart was breaking.

15.   When Jesus was led by the Spirit into the wilderness, He was tempted to serve Himself, and thereby Satan. What was His response to this temptation according to Matthew 4:10?

16.   We too are tempted to serve ourselves or our own interests. Does this mean it is wrong to take care of our needs? Why or why not?

17.   What does the Lord proclaim in Jeremiah 2:11? What do you think the real issue is? How do you think the Lord feels when His people act this way?

18. Of the key elements of worship—adoring, thanking, and praising—which comes easiest for you? Which is most difficult? Why do you think this is true?

19. As we have seen, worship brings us into God's presence and reveals His glory. Foster says, "To worship is to experience reality, to touch Life. It is to know, to feel, to experience the resurrected Christ."[9] Set aside a block of time now for worship. Use the following ideas as a guide to worship:

- Focus on the Lord and who He is. Read Psalm 95:1-7 and Colossians 1:15-20.
- Restate the truths of these passages as your personalized adoration.
- If you have a hymnal or song book, read (or sing) a favorite hymn or song of praise such as "Crown Him with Many Crowns" or "Great Is Thy Faithfulness."
- Music is a wonderful tool for praise and worship! Play your favorite tape or CD as you continue in worship.
- Like the psalmist declares in 100:1-4, praise God for who He is. Thank Him for what He has done and promises to do.
- Use Psalms 100:5, 139:1-16, and 145 as springboards for praise. Reflect on who God is and adore Him! Record your expressions.
- Reflect on God's unconditional love for you as expressed in Romans 8:38-39.
- Praise God for how you have seen His love, goodness, faithfulness, and grace specifically in your life. Recount these here or in your journal.
- If you have a particular sorrow or difficult situation, offer a sacrifice of praise based on what you *know* is true of God and His concern for you.
- Ask the Father to open your eyes to see His faithfulness.
- Thank God for all that He does. Reflect on Psalms 23, 32, 86:5-13, and Ephesians 1:3-14.

- Read or sing a song of thankfulness such as "Amazing Grace" or "What a Friend We Have in Jesus."
- Express your thanksgiving to God for what He has specifically done for you and given to you. Bask in His goodness and faithfulness.
- Offer yourself to the Lord as an expression of worship and love. Ask Him to fulfill His purposes in you and for you.
- Be still before God as you offer yourself to Him. Express your love to Him and enjoy Him!

20. In what ways, if any, has your concept of worship changed from before beginning this chapter?

Between You and God

21. Read again Richard Foster's thoughts on the results of worship on page 80. To what new level of obedience do you feel the Lord is calling you?

22. a. Consider Colossians 3:17,23-24. What tasks can you transform into acts of worship?

b. What differences would this make in what you do and how well you do it? Be specific.

23.   In closing, according to Psalm 115:1, what should our heart's
       desire be at all times and in all things? Express your heart to the
       Lord now.

       As we worship, we are led into service and our service itself becomes
an act of worship. This continues throughout each day as we practice
praise and adoration. As you go through your day, be sensitive to His Spirit
as He prompts you to worship. Whether it is a song on the radio, the beauty
of His creation, or the expression of His love through another person, don't
give in to the temptation to rush on. Take time to worship and enjoy Him.
It delights Him and refreshes you.

CHAPTER TEN

Ever-Increasing Intimacy

Like an apple tree among the trees of the forest is my lover among the
young men. I delight to sit in his shade, and his fruit is sweet to my taste.
He has taken me to the banquet hall, and his banner over me is love.

— Song of Songs 2:3-4

"I am the good shepherd; I know my sheep and my sheep know me – just
as the Father knows me and I know the Father.... As the Father has
loved me, so have I loved you. Now remain in my love."

— John 10:14-15; 15:9

Y OU are deeply loved by God. You were in His heart before He created
the world or formed you in the womb. He created you for a love relationship with Himself and He calls you to an ever-increasing intimacy
of mutual delight. He calls you into oneness with Himself!

In his book *The Life of the Beloved,* Henri Nouwen states, "The unfath-
omable mystery of God is that God is a Lover who wants to be loved.
The One who created us is waiting for our response to the love that gave
us our being."[1]

Nouwen says he wants *you* "to claim for yourself the truth spoken
by the voice that says, 'You are my Beloved.' . . . Every time you listen with
great attentiveness to the voice that calls you the Beloved, you will discover within yourself a desire to hear that voice longer and more deeply.
It is like discovering a well in the desert."[2]

As we conclude this study, we will expand on the basics of relationship from chapter two. Then we will focus on the depth of intimacy to
which the Lord calls us.

Time in God's Word

We have come full circle in our study. In chapter one we identified the one thing that is needed—to sit at the Lord's feet. Jesus commended Mary not only because she would benefit, but also because He enjoyed her company. Each chapter has presented biblical principles and practical tools for establishing and building a love relationship with our Lord. We will conclude as we began—sitting at Jesus' feet.

1. In any relationship, how does one grow closer to the other? How does this relate to your relationship with the Lord? Explain.

2. Based on 2 Timothy 3:15-16, what is a key to getting to know God better?

3. The better we get to know God, the more we love Him. According to Matthew 22:37-38, what does the Lord desire from us?

4. Besides through His Word, how do God and His people communicate with each other? (See Luke 11:9-10 and Philippians 4:4-7.)

While God desires intimacy with all of us, not all of us experience the same intense intimacy with Him. According to J. Oswald Sanders, the level of intimacy each of us attains with God has much to do with us and our response to God's desire:

In both Old and New Testaments, there are examples of four

degrees of intimacy experienced by God's people. . . . [Regarding Jesus and His disciples] there ended up to be four circles: the seventy; the twelve; the three; and then one. . . . Each of the disciples was as close to Jesus as he chose to be, for the Son of God had no favorites. . . . Their relationship with Him was the result of their own choice, conscious or unconscious. It is a sobering thought that we too are as close to Christ as we really choose to be . . . It would seem that admission to the inner circle of deepening intimacy with God is the outcome of *deep desire*.[3]

5. In what specific ways might the degree or intensity of one's desire toward God be evidenced?

6. As you do desire to be closer to Him, what does the Lord promise you in Jeremiah 30:21-22?

7. According to Jesus' words in John 15:9-10, if we desire to be close to Him, what must we do? Why did Jesus share this information? (See verse 11.)

8. What is the relationship between obedience and oneness with Christ? Like the proverbial question of the chicken and the egg, which came first—the obedience or the oneness? Explain your response.

9. In the verses below, what images does Jesus use to illustrate the

increasing intimacy He desires with us? What are the similarities and differences between these three types of relationships?

a. Matthew 9:15 and 25:1

b. John 15:13-15

c. 1 John 3:1

10.   For each type of love relationship in question 9, give an example of what each party might do to please the other. As our love for the Lord grows, how is this also seen in that relationship? If you love the Lord, how are you showing Him?

11.   Let's look deeper into the imagery of marriage as a picture of our love relationship with the Lord. What do you learn from Hosea 2:16,19-20 and Revelation 19:6-9? What aspect of His vow is particularly meaningful to you and why?

12.   What incredible statement is made in Ephesians 5:31-32? What are your responses to this truth?

Brent Curtis and John Eldredge, authors of *The Sacred Romance,* share helpful insights on the depth of God's love and His desire for our love:

Indeed, if we will listen, a Sacred Romance calls to us. . . . Something calls to us through experiences [of both joys and sorrows] and rouses an inconsolable longing deep within our heart, wakening in us a yearning for intimacy, beauty, and adventure. . . . And the voice that calls to us in this place is none other than the voice of God. . . . Above all else, the Christian life is a love affair of the heart. . . . [4]

From the beginning, we know that God is a lover at heart, from all eternity. . . . The Scriptures employ a wide scale of metaphors to capture the many facets of our relationship with God . . . [servants, children, friends]. . . . But there is still a higher and deeper level of intimacy and partnership awaiting us at the top of this metaphorical ascent. We are lovers. . . . "As a bridegroom rejoices over his bride, so will I rejoice over you," so that we might say in return, "I am my beloved's and his desire is for me."

The heart-cry of every soul [is] for intimacy with God. For this we were created and for this we were rescued from sin and death. . . . God loved us before the beginning of time, has come for us, and now calls us to journey toward him, with him, for the consummation of our love.[5]

13. What are your thoughts, questions, and responses as you reflect on these incredible truths?

As our love for Him deepens, our desire grows from simply wanting to please Him in all we *do*—to desiring to *be* pleasing to Him! Amy Carmichael, British missionary to India and author of more than forty books, expressed the essence of this desire in her prayer, "O Lord Jesus, my Beloved, let me be a joy to Thee."[6]

14.   Reflect on Malachi 3:2-3 and Hebrews 12:10-11. As we desire to be a joy to our Lord and grow closer to Him, what does the Lord do? Why is this necessary?

15.   What will be the result of God's loving discipline according to Job 23:10? How does this deepen our union with Him?

    Henri Nouwen explains how joy can come out of sorrow. He writes, "This [result of discipline] explains why true joy can be experienced in the midst of great suffering. It is the joy of being disciplined, purified, and pruned. Just as athletes who experience great pain as they run the race can, at the same time, taste the joy of knowing that they are coming closer to their goal, so also can the Beloved experience suffering as a way to the deeper communion for which they yearn."[7]

16.   How does this understanding affect your perspective on any heartaches or difficulties you are presently experiencing?

17.   Before His death and resurrection, Jesus promised His disciples they would not be left alone because He would send a Counselor (John 14:15-18). Even though all believers have the Holy Spirit, what are we commanded to do in Ephesians 5:18? Why is this important?

18.	Often when we think of the Holy Spirit we think of power and greater effectiveness. Reflect for a moment on the truth that He is the *Holy* Spirit and He lives in us if we have trusted Christ for forgiveness of sin. What insights about oneness does this fact give you?

BETWEEN YOU AND ME

Today Christ Himself and His love are my greatest joys! His love thrills me to the depths of my soul and lifts me to the heights. Being with Him is my greatest pleasure. I ache for people who choose not to pursue this love relationship. Yet I have not always had this perspective.

Early in the Christian life, believers often thrill most over the gifts God gives them and the things He does for them. We can be like little children when grandparents arrive. Frequently the child's first question is, "What did you bring me?" The excitement is over the gift. But as they grow, children realize that the gift is really the person who has come to be with them. So it is in the Christian life. As we mature, we discover that Christ Himself is His greatest gift.

As in any love relationship, the joy in being together is mutual. In *The Perfect Love*, Ruth Myers writes of God's delight in us:

Perhaps you easily remember that God has compassion for you and is willing to help you. . . . But maybe you've overlooked how intense His feelings really are—how He desires you, how much He finds delight whenever you cultivate your love relationship with Him as one who belongs to Him. . . . What better motivation can there be for spending time with Him day by day?[8]

19.	What impact does this love relationship with the Lord have on other relationships we may have? What would be the outworking of the truths in the following verses?

a. 1 Corinthians 13:4-7

b. Galatians 5:22-23

c. Ephesians 3:16-19

Reflection and Application
20.   What heart response do you have as you reflect on the truth that *you* bring the Lord joy as you love Him and delight in being with Him?

21.   For some, the fact that Christ is not physically present has proven to be a stumbling block in nurturing a relationship with Him as Bridegroom or Husband. What struggles do you have with this, or any other, dimension of God's heart? Express your heart to Him here or in your journal.

22.   If you experience internal resistance to pursuing a more intimate relationship with Jesus Christ, be honest with the Lord. As much as the Lord desires intimacy with you, He will not violate

your free will by pushing past barriers you have erected to keep Him away. Let Him reveal any of these walls such as lack of trust, hurt, or fear. Journal your feelings to Him and ask Him to meet you in them.

Because God reveals Himself through His Word, take all the time in the Word that you need to grasp the reality of His love for you. Skim the Gospel of John for His words of love. Browse the Song of Solomon for a picture of God as Lover and Husband. As Warren Wiersbe says, "The better we know the Word of God, the better we shall know the God of the Word."[9]

23.   Reflect on the passages below and jot down any special insights God gives you.

   a. Song of Songs 2:8

   b. Song of Songs 2:14

   c. 1 John 4:18

Henri Nouwen writes, "God not only says: 'You are my Beloved.' God also asks: 'Do you love me?' . . . At every point of the journey there is the choice to say 'Yes' and the choice to say 'No.'"[10] What choice will you make today?

24.   The maiden in the Song of Songs said a whole-hearted *yes* to the Lord. The results she experienced are what the Lord desires for us as well.

a. What does the maiden say she enjoys in 1:2-3 and 2:3-4? Take time now to "sit in his shade" and taste of the fruit of all that He is. Enjoy Him and praise Him.

b. At times He seemed distant to the maiden. According to 3:1-4, what did she do during those times, and what resulted? Why do you think the Lord at times seems to hide Himself?

c. How does the Lord delight in the maiden's love according to 4:1,7-15 and 6:4-9? What is the essence of these passages as they pertain to your relationship with Him?

d. What is the beloved assured of in 7:10? Are you aware of this as well? Write your requests here to the Lord and seek truth through His Word.

In his commentary *Song of Songs*, Watchman Nee encourages us: "As soon as the experience of the inner chamber begins, there is a surge of satisfaction in the thought of a life of love with the King, who is also a Bridegroom-Lover. [Those who desire this intimate relationship] right well know that God will perfect what He has begun to do in them."[11] Hang on to this assurance as your hunger for Him deepens.

Receive now the love of the Lord. Picture the look of love in His eyes

as you, His bride, approach and respond to His love. Let His love pene-
trate and saturate your soul, your entire being. Let it fill you and flow over
you—and then through you to those around you. Savor His love and
delight in Him. Celebrate Him and His love for you. Know He receives
your love and takes joy in your expression.

BETWEEN YOU AND ME

When we walk with Him in obedience, God's love and joy are so
abundant, they fill us beyond capacity. God gave me a visual picture of this while I was visiting Milwaukee. In the downtown area,
I saw a wonderful multilevel fountain. As the water filled the first
level, it overflowed and cascaded to the other levels. It was beau-
tiful and inspiring. As I watched this fountain, the Lord reminded
me of how He fills me and all believers with His love and the joy
of His presence. He gives in such abundance that it cannot be con-
tained. As a result His joy and love overflow to others.

As this study of *At Jesus' Feet* ends, consider God's loving call to you.
It begins with, "Come to Me and sit at My feet." Like Mary, this is the
one thing *you* need. He also calls you to an ever-deepening intimacy with
Him—to a oneness, a union that satisfies your soul and delights His heart.
As this oneness develops, He also calls you to go into the world with His
love and good news. The natural overflow of life in Christ is to tell others who He is and what He has done for you.

Chapter One—Recognizing the One Thing
1. Deborah Newman, *Then God Created Woman* (Colorado Springs, Colo.: Focus on the Family, 1997), pp. 199-200.
2. Ruth Myers, *31 Days of Praise* (Sisters, Ore.: Questar, 1994), p. 138.
3. A. W. Tozer, *The Best of Tozer, Volume 2,* comp. Warren W. Wiersbe (Lincoln, Neb.: Baker Book House, 1978; Camp Hill, Penn.: Christian Publications, 1995), p. 149.
4. Oswald Chambers, *My Utmost for His Highest,* ed. James Reimann (Grand Rapids, Mich.: Oswald Chambers Publications Assn., Ltd.; Grand Rapids, Mich.: Discovery House Publishers, 1992), May 25.
5. To learn more about this concept, see my book *The Responsive Heart* (Colorado Springs, Colo.: NavPress, 2000). An entire chapter of this book is devoted to these truths.
6. Ruth Myers, *The Perfect Love* (Colorado Springs, Colo.: WaterBrook Press, 1998), p. 26.

Chapter Two—Building in the Basics
1. A. W. Tozer, *The Best of Tozer, Volume 2,* comp. Warren W. Wiersbe (Lincoln, Neb.: Baker Book House, 1978; Camp Hill, Penn.: Christian Publications, 1995), pp. 14-15.

Chapter Three—Feeding on God's Word
1. Jerry Bridges, *Transforming Grace* (Colorado Springs, Colo.: NavPress, 1991), p. 177.
2. A. W. Tozer, *The Best of Tozer, Volume 2,* comp. Warren W. Wiersbe (Lincoln, Neb.: Baker Book House, 1978; Camp Hill, Penn.: Christian Publications, 1995), p. 26.
3. Tozer, p. 108.
4. Andrew Murray, *The Inner Life* (New Kensington, Pa.: Whitaker House, 1984), p. 36.
5. Tozer, p. 108.
6. Murray, p. 41.

Chapter Four—Dialoguing Through Prayer: Part One
1. Deborah Newman, *Then God Created Woman* (Colorado Springs, Colo.: Focus on the Family, 1997), p. 271.
2. Lloyd John Ogilvie, *Praying with Power* (Ventura, Calif.: Regal, 1983, 1988), p. 27.
3. Bill Bright, *Ten Basic Steps Toward Christian Maturity* (San Bernardino, Calif.: Campus Crusade for Christ, 1972), p. 244.
4. Ogilvie, p. 27.
5. Richard Foster, *Celebration of Discipline: The Path to Spiritual Growth* (New York: HarperCollins Publishers, Inc., 1978), pp. 30-31.

Chapter Five—Dialoguing Through Prayer: Part Two
1. Colin Whittaker, *Seven Guides to Effective Prayer* (Minneapolis, Minn.: Bethany, 1987), pp. 83-84.

Chapter Six—Listening to the Spirit
1. Richard Foster, *Celebration of Discipline: The Path to Spiritual Growth* (New York: HarperCollins Publishers, Inc., 1978), p. 34.
2. Lloyd John Ogilvie, *Praying with Power* (Ventura, Calif.: Regal, 1983, 1988), p. 25.
3. Andrew Murray, *The Inner Life* (New Kensington, Pa.: Whitaker House, 1984), pp. 66-68.

Chapter Seven—Perservering When God is Silent
1. Oswald Chambers, *My Utmost for His Highest,* ed. James Reimann (Grand Rapids, Mich.: Oswald Chambers Publications Assn., Ltd.; Grand Rapids, Mich.: Discovery House Publishers, 1992), September 12.
2. Richard Foster, *Celebration of Discipline: The Path to Spiritual Growth* (New York: HarperCollins Publishers, Inc., 1978), pp. 89-90.
3. Watchman Nee, *The Normal Christian Life* (Wheaton, Ill.: Tyndale, 1977), pp. 263-265.

Chapter Eight—Growing Through Fasting and Feasting
1. Richard Foster, *Celebration of Discipline: The Path to Spiritual Growth* (New York: HarperCollins Publishers, Inc., 1978), p. 44.
2. Foster, pp. 42-44.
3. Foster, p. 44.
4. Bill Bright, *The Coming Revival* (Orlando, Fla.: NewLife Publications, Campus Crusade for Christ, 1995), pp. 98-99.
5. Dr. Wesley L. Duewel, *Mighty Prevailing Power* (Grand Rapids, Mich.: Zondervan, 1990; Greenwood, Ind.: Duewel Literature Trust, Inc., 1990), p. 181.
6. Foster, p. 48.
7. Duewel, p. 182.
8. Foster, p. 45.
9. Foster, p. 43.
10. Foster, p. 43.
11. Bright, *The Coming Revival*, p. 123.
12. Bill Bright, *The Transforming Power of Fasting and Prayer* (Orlando, Fla.: NewLife Publications, Campus Crusade for Christ, 1997), pp. 30-31.
13. Duewel, pp. 192-193.
14. Bright, *The Transforming Power of Fasting and Prayer*, p. 165; and *The Coming Revival*, p. 92.
15. Henri J. M. Nouwen, *The Return of the Prodigal Son* (New York: Doubleday, 1992), pp. 105-106.

Chapter Nine—Enjoying God in Worship
1. Warren Wiersbe, *Real Worship* (Nashville, Tenn.: Thomas-Nelson, 1986), pp. 21-22.
2. A. W. Tozer, *The Best of Tozer, Volume 2*, comp. Warren W. Wiersbe (Lincoln, Neb.: Baker Book House, 1978; Camp Hill, Penn.: Christian Publications, 1995), p. 221.
3. Dr. Wesley L. Duewel, *Mighty Prevailing Power* (Grand Rapids, Mich.: Zondervan, 1990; Greenwood, Ind.: Duewel Literature Trust, Inc., 1990), p. 169.
2. Ruth Myers, *31 Days of Praise* (Sisters, Ore.: Questar, 1994), pp. 123, 144.
5. Myers, p. 140.
6. Myers, pp. 34, 150.
7. Wiersbe, pp. 30-31.
5. Richard Foster, *Celebration of Discipline: The Path to Spiritual Growth* (New York: HarperCollins Publishers, Inc., 1978), p. 148.
9. Foster, p. 138.

Chapter Ten—Ever-Increasing Intimacy
1. Henri Nouwen, *The Life of the Beloved* (New York: Crossroad Publishing Company, 1992), p. 106.
2. Nouwen, pp. 30-31.
3. J. Oswald Sanders, *Enjoying Intimacy with God* (Chicago: Moody, 1980), pp. 12-18.
4. Brent Curtis and John Eldredge, *The Sacred Romance* (Nashville, Tenn.: Thomas Nelson, 1997), pp. 6-8.
5. Curtis and Eldredge, pp. 74, 96-97.
6. Amy Carmichael, *Rose from Brier* (Fort Washington, Pa.: Christian Literature Crusade, 1992), p. 87.
7. Nouwen, p. 80.
8. Ruth Myers, *The Perfect Love* (Colorado Springs, Colo.: WaterBrook Press, 1998), pp. 26, 34-35.
9. Warren Wiersbe, *Real Worship* (Nashville, Tenn.: Thomas-Nelson, 1986), p. 61.
10. Nouwen, pp. 106-107.
11. Watchman Nee, *Song of Songs* (Fort Washington, Pa.: Christian Literature Crusade, 1972), p. 21.

DATE DUE